Social Networking
Marketing Opportunities and Challenges

By
Smita Sharma

CONTENT

LIST OF FIGURES

LIST OF TABLES

Abstract

Introduction to the Study

This research aims to establish an understanding of use of social networking sites by Indian consumers and organizations. The first part of the study aims to identify the profile of Indian consumers who use social networking sites. Further, it also examines the relationship between consumer engagement and electronic word of mouth. In today's fragmented media landscape, generating positive word of mouth among consumers has become an important tool for marketers. Marketers are challenged with identifying influential individuals in social networks and connecting with them in ways that encourage word of mouth message movement.

As more and more marketers attempt to harness the power of electronic word of mouth in social networking sites (Williamson, 2006), rigorous investigation of determinants that lead to consumers' engagement in electronic word of mouth via the social networks is becoming critical. A central question to answer is what factors influence electronic word of mouth behavior in social networking sites and what are the underlying processes of electronic word of mouth communications in this new social medium.

A major study in the present research focuses on five social relationship variables: social capital, tie strength, homophily, trust, and interpersonal influence that are all related to electronic word of mouth behavior in social networking sites. Despite the highly social nature of social networking sites, little is known about the potential drivers that lead to consumers' reliance on electronic word of mouth occurring via these sites.

The research aims to provide a theoretical understanding of consumers' use of social networking sites as a vehicle for electronic word of mouth. Specifically, the current study attempts to empirically examine potential roles of social factors in electronic word of mouth via social networking sites. This study examines whether existing research on word of mouth developed in the traditional marketplace can be applied to the new medium, social networking sites, and contributes to the literature on computer-mediated communication with specific emphasis on online social media. Managerially, understanding social relationship variables that affect consumers' electronic word of mouth behaviors could help marketers to identify influential individuals in personal networks and to effectively generate and manage positive electronic word of mouth communication. At the same time, findings from this research could provide marketers with valuable information to establish and strengthen their long-term relationships with consumers in social networking sites and use beneficial electronic word of mouth to promote selected brands.

Companies deploy online social networks, platforms, tools and services in various activities aiming to create better experience for consumers which can lead to loyalty, better branding and increase of sales.

The second part of the study aims to analyze the usage of social networking sites in marketing communication programs implemented by brands and organizations. Facebook has emerged as the most important platform for marketers in India, followed by Twitter, YouTube and Blogging. Being a popular social media platform in India, Facebook is the favorite playground for social media-savvy organizations in India to engage in everyday conversations and organize engaging promotions and contests for fans.

The study summarizes empirical evidence of frequency of usage, budgeting, purposes of use and metrics of evaluation, with respect to social networks within different organizations.

Marketers need to devise new purposes and metrics for use and evaluation, on the basis of changing market dynamics. Social media adoption should be seen as a cultural and behavioral shift within the organization to transparently engage with customers who are not afraid to voice their opinions and are big influencers to their connected networks.

Chapter 1

Introduction

Introduction

Chapter Overview

This chapter highlights the importance and growth of social networking sites worldwide and its importance in marketing communication. It outlines the use of social networking sites by Indian consumers and companies. It discusses the rationale behind the present research and gives an overview of the objectives of the present study.

In the end, the chapter provides an outline of the thesis.

1.1 Background of the Study

Internet penetration in the country may not have crossed 16% of the population yet, but in absolute numbers, this percentage works out to nearly 10 times the population of Australia. A report released by the Internet and Mobile Association of India (IAMAI)[1] and IMRB International[2] estimated 243 million internet users in the country by mid-2014, overtaking the US as the world's second largest internet base after China.

While Indians primarily use the internet for communication, largely in the form of email, social media is also an important driver of internet use in India. This facet of the IAMAI report can be corroborated with data from other sources such as Forbes; and Facebook[3], the world's largest social media company, which crossed 114 million active users in India — the second country, after the United States.

Previously, it was enough to have an online presence on the Internet for the one-way broadcasting and dissemination of information. Today, social networks such as Facebook and micro blogging sites like Twitter are driving new forms of social interaction, dialogue, exchange and collaboration. Social networking sites (referred to more broadly as social

---

[1] Internet & Mobile Association of India is a not-for-profit industry body registered under the Societies Act, 1986. Its mandate is to expand and enhance the online and mobile value added services sectors.

[2] IMRB International is a multi-country market research, survey and business consultancy firm that offers a range of syndicated data and customized research services.

[3] Facebook is a social utility that connects people with friends and others who work, study and live around them.

media) enable users to swap ideas, post updates and comments, or participate in activities and events, while sharing their wider interests. From general chit-chat to propagating breaking news, from scheduling a date to following election results or coordinating disaster response, from gentle humour to serious research, social networks are now used for a host of different reasons by various user communities.

A social networking service is a platform to build social networks or social relations among people who, for example, share interests, activities, backgrounds, or real-life connections. A social network service consists of a representation of each user (often a profile), his/her social links, and a variety of additional services. Most social network services are web-based and provide means for users to interact over the Internet, such as e-mail and instant messaging. Online community services are sometimes considered as a social network service, though in a broader sense, social network service usually means an individual-centered service whereas online community services are group-centered. Social networking sites allow users to share ideas, pictures, posts, activities, events, and interests with people in their network.

Social networking sites have different rules for establishing connections, but they often allow users to view the connections of a confirmed connection and even suggest further connections based on a person's established network. Some social networking websites like LinkedIn[4] are used for establishing professional connections, while sites like Facebook straddle the line between private and professional. There are also many networks that are built for a specific user base, such as cultural or political groups within a given area or even traders in financial markets.

From beginning of their introduction, social networking sites have attracted millions of users, many of whom have integrated these sites into their daily practices. There are hundreds of social networking sites, with various technological affordances, supporting a wide range of interests and practices. While their key technological features are fairly consistent, the cultures that emerge around social networking sites are varied. Most sites support the maintenance of pre-existing social networks, but others help strangers connect based on shared interests, political views, or activities. Some sites cater to diverse

[4] LinkedIn is the social network for work professionals created by Reid Hoffman in 2002.

audiences, while others attract people based on common language or shared racial, sexual, religious, or nationality-based identities. Sites also vary in the extent to which they incorporate new information and communication tools, such as mobile connectivity, blogging, and photo/video-sharing.

According to Boyd and Ellison's (2007) article, "Why Youth (Heart) Social Network Sites: The Role of Networked Publics in Teenage Social Life", social networking sites share a variety of technical features that allow individuals to: construct a public/semi-public profile, articulate a list of other users that they share a connection with, and view their list of connections within the system. The most basic of these are visible profiles with a list of "friends" who are also users of the site. In an article entitled "Social Network Sites: Definition, History, and Scholarship," Boyd and Ellison adopted Sunden's (2003) description of profiles as unique pages where one can "type oneself into being".

A profile is generated from answers to questions, such as age, location, interests, etc. Some sites allow users to upload pictures, add multimedia content or modify the look and feel of the profile. Others, e.g., Facebook, allow users to enhance their profile by adding modules or "Applications". Many sites allow users to post blog entries, search for others with similar interests and compile and share lists of contacts. User profiles often have a section dedicated to comments from friends and other users. To protect user privacy, social networks typically have controls that allow users to choose who can view their profile, contact them, add them to their list of contacts, and so on.

Some social networks have additional features, such as the ability to create groups that share common interests or affiliations, upload or stream live videos, and hold discussions in forums. Geo-social networking co-opts Internet mapping services to organize user participation around geographic features and their attributes.

Companies have found that social networking sites such as Facebook and LinkedIn are great ways to build their brand image. According to Jody Nimetz, author of "Marketing Jive", there are five major uses for businesses and social media: to create brand awareness, as an online reputation management tool, for recruiting, to learn about new technologies and competitors, and as a lead generation tool to intercept potential prospects. These companies are able to drive traffic to their own online sites while encouraging their consumers and clients to have discussions on how to improve or change products or services.

Today, social networking services have become a mainstream topic of academic study in various disciplines. For example, social networking services are highly relevant to techno self studies which focus on all aspects of human identity in a technological society.

Social networking services are not just bringing Internet users into fast-flowing online conversations — social media are helping people to follow breaking news, keep up with friends or colleagues, contribute to online debates or learn from others. They are transforming online user behavior in terms of users' initial entry point, search, browsing and purchasing behavior. Some experts suggest that social media will become the Internet's new search function -predicting that people will spend less time navigating the Internet independently and instead search for information or make decisions based on "word-of-mouth" recommendations from their friends, the so-called "friend-casting".

Social networking sites have brought a revolution in communication among people and within organizations.
The recent development of web 2.0 technologies and social networks brought enormous possibilities for consumers and companies. The number of online social users has grown very fast in recent years and socialization became most important activity for the internet users. There are a number of determinants including social factors which affect the socialization in social networking sites.

This research aims to establish an understanding of use of social networking sites by Indian consumers and organizations. The first part of the study aims to identify the profile of Indian consumers who use social networking sites. Further, it also examines the relationship between consumer engagement and electronic word of mouth.

In today's fragmented media landscape, generating positive word of mouth among consumers has become an important tool for marketers. Marketers are challenged with identifying influential individuals in social networks and connecting with them in ways that encourage word of mouth message movement.

As more and more marketers attempt to harness the power of electronic word of mouth in social networking sites (Williamson, 2006), rigorous investigation of determinants that lead to consumers' engagement in electronic word of mouth via the social networks is becoming critical. A central question to answer is what factors influence electronic word of mouth behavior in social networking sites and what are the underlying processes of electronic word of mouth communications in this new social medium.

A major study in the present research focuses on five social relationship variables: social capital, tie strength, homophily, trust, and interpersonal influence that are all related to electronic word of mouth behavior in social networking sites. Despite the highly social nature of social networking sites, little is known about the potential drivers that lead to consumers' reliance on electronic word of mouth occurring via these sites.

The research aims to provide a theoretical understanding of consumers' use of social networking sites as a vehicle for electronic word of mouth. Specifically, the current study attempts to empirically examine potential roles of social factors in electronic word of mouth via social networking sites. This study examines whether existing research on word of mouth developed in the traditional marketplace can be applied to the new medium, social networking sites, and contributes to the literature on computer-mediated communication with specific emphasis on online social media. Managerially, understanding social relationship variables that affect consumers' electronic word of mouth behaviors could help marketers to identify influential individuals in personal networks and to effectively generate and manage positive electronic word of mouth communication. At the same time, findings from this research could provide marketers with valuable information to establish and strengthen their long-term relationships with consumers in social networking sites and use beneficial electronic word of mouth to promote selected brands.

Companies deploy online social networks, platforms, tools and services in various activities aiming to create better experience for consumers which can lead to loyalty, better branding and increase of sales.

The second part of the study aims to analyze the usage of social networking sites in marketing communication programs implemented by brands and organizations.

Facebook has emerged as the most important platform for marketers in India, followed by Twitter, YouTube and Blogging.

Being a popular social media platform in India, Facebook is the favorite playground for social media-savvy organizations in India to engage in everyday conversations and organize engaging promotions and contests for fans.

The study summarizes empirical evidence of frequency of usage, budgeting, purposes of use and metrics of evaluation, with respect to social networks within different organizations.

Marketers need to devise new purposes and metrics for use and evaluation, on the basis of changing market dynamics. Social media adoption should be seen as a cultural and behavioral shift within the organization to transparently engage with customers who are not afraid to voice their opinions and are big influencers to their connected networks.

1.2 Social Networking Sites: An Overview

A social networking service is an online service, platform, or site that focuses on facilitating the building of social networks or social relations among people who, for example, share interests, activities, backgrounds, or real-life connections. A social network service consists of a representation of each user (often a profile), his/her social links, and a variety of additional services. Most social network services are web-based and provide means for users to interact over the Internet, such as e-mail and instant messaging. Online community services are sometimes considered as a social network service, though in a broader sense, social network service usually means an individual-centered service whereas online community services are group-centered. Social networking sites allow users to share ideas, activities, events, and interests within their individual networks.

Social networking, as defined for the online world, is about forming communities of shared interest, and giving people in those communities, tools to come together, communicate with each other, and produce meaningful content that is important to them. Online social networks allow people to dramatically expand their personal social networks, finding others with shared interests or values. Social networks also provide the tools for their members to become content producers, facilitating user-submitted photos, videos, blogs, multimedia, reviews, etc. Their members share of themselves with their personal social networking communities, becoming publishers by participating.

The "content" that is on a social network does not come from the publisher, it comes from the users themselves -- and their interaction is a major portion of the content. What the social network operator brings to the table is the publishing and personal-communications tools, plus management and oversight to keep the community in order.
As Boyd and Ellison (2007) defined, social networking sites are web-based services that allow individuals to construct a public profile and articulate a list of their contacts with which they share a social network. Social networking sites provide an effective, powerful channel for consumers to create a visible personal profile, build a personal network, and display interpersonal commentaries publicly (Lenhart and Madden, 2007). Without geographic and time constraints, consumers can easily and quickly exchange product-related information and opinions with their personal contacts (Graham and Havlena, 2007) and have the potential to reach global audiences who share common interests in a product or brand.

With the new applications on social networking sites, the way consumers make purchase decisions and interact with members of their social network has fundamentally changed (Hung and Li 2007; Niederhoffer *et al.,* 2007). Social networking sites not only enhance consumers' online experiences, but also change their online expectations (e.g., social and information outcomes). For example, activities occurring in social networking sites range from socializing with existing friends or making new ones to exchanging information and experiences regarding products or services. All of these online communications have potentially led consumers to change their approach to searching for product information and making purchase decisions.

Social networking sites are increasingly attracting the attention of academic and industry researchers intrigued by their affordances and reach. Since their introduction, social network sites have attracted millions of users, many of whom have integrated these sites into their daily practices. There are hundreds of social networking sites, with various technological affordances, supporting a wide range of interests and practices. While their key technological features are fairly consistent, the cultures that emerge around social networking sites are varied. Most sites support the maintenance of pre-existing social networks, but others help strangers connect based on shared interests, political views, or activities. Some sites cater to diverse audiences, while others attract people based on common language or shared racial, sexual, religious, or nationality-based identities. Sites also vary in the extent to which they incorporate new information and communication tools, such as mobile connectivity, blogging, and photo/video-sharing.

The rapid growth of social networking that has been observed over the last two to three years is indicative of its entry into the mainstream culture and its integration into the daily lives of many people. In parallel with this, there has also been considerable media coverage of the growth of social networking, its potential positive outcomes and concerns about the way that some people are engaging with it.

The next section provides an overview of the prevalence of social networking sites as well as the current brand activities on these sites.

Prevalence of Social Networking Sites

Growth in the number of social network users around the world may be slowing, but it shows little sign of stopping, based on eMarketer's latest forecast of internet, broadband and social network users worldwide.

As per eMarketer[5], 1.61 billion people logged in to social networking sites at least monthly, from any electronic device in the year 2013. There was a 14.2% gain on social networker numbers from 2012, and double-digit growth is expected to continue for another year. By 2017, 2.33 billion people will use social networks.

Currently, the highest penetration of social network users as a share of total population occurs in the Netherlands, where 63.5% of all residents are social network users; Norway follows just behind at 63.3%. Majorities of residents in Sweden, South Korea, Denmark, the US, Finland, Canada and the UK also use social networking sites monthly.

[5] eMarketer is an independent market research company that provides insights and trends related to digital marketing, media and commerce.

Brand Activities on Social Networking Sites

As social networking sites have become a prevailing communication technology in the evolution of the digital era for today's Internet users (Ipsos[6] Insight, 2007), marketers strive to use this online social medium to gain competitive advantage, increase brand awareness, create brand loyalty, and establish long-term relationships with their potential consumers. To help marketers target their consumers more effectively, different advertising formats have been developed by leading social networking sites. For example, Facebook advertisements consist of three dimensions, including branded profile pages (i.e. virtual communities), social advertisements, and beacons.

First, branded profile pages, like online brand communities, allow marketers to create specific pages where consumers can register as members and show their commitment to the brand (Morrissey, 2007). Second, social advertisements enhance consumer involvement by encouraging them to participate in activities such as passing along promotional messages to their friends, similar to electronic word of mouth based viral marketing.

Lastly, drawing from the concept of customer-relationship management (CRM), by using beacons, Facebook tracks consumer purchase behavior, utilizes the information to identify valuable customers, and delivers relevant messages to them. These advertising mechanisms in networking platforms facilitate marketers' implementation of advertising campaigns in social networking sites. As a result, a growing number of marketers are turning to online social medium to promote their brands to the highly-engaged consumers.

Due to the potential of social networking sites for brand communication among consumers and consumer-brand relationships, advertising spending on social networking sites has undergone tremendous growth. With the rapid growth in the popularity of social networking sites, academic research has examined users' usage patterns, self-presentation strategies, motivations, and social relationships associated with this relatively new online communication medium and provided an initial understanding of the phenomenon (e.g., Choi *et al.,* 2008; Ellison, Steinfield, and Lampe, 2007; Jung, Youn, and Mcclung, 2007).

More important to marketers is the huge potential of social networking sites to connect a

[6] Ipsos is a global market research company with worldwide headquarters in Paris, France.

vast number of prospective consumers around the world. The extensive social interactions among many consumers through their public personal networks have created an information-intensive environment of social networking sites where consumers can easily and quickly disseminate their thoughts and opinions. For this reason, social networking sites can play a significant role in sharing and distributing product-related information, and can serve as an influential vehicle for electronic word of mouth.

1.3 Social Networking Sites- Consumers' Perspective

Social media is an essential touch point in today's consumer decision process, from stage quo to the stage of post purchase; likewise, companies are engaging with the purpose of creating brand awareness, engaging their existing customers, driving traffic to other marketing properties and growing channel number.

Each of the social media platforms plays a role in giving out, receiving, and exchanging information without any boundary limitations, and enables two-way flow of information. Since the flow of communication does not merely impact how companies can access their targeted groups, but also it influences throughout the entire decision process, from interpreting the message, searching for available alternatives, as well as actions carried out in the after the purchase; thus, it is important to denote that message rejection, misinterpretation, and misunderstanding are the possible pitfalls in the flow of communication.

In relation to social media, the biggest fear of companies and brands is to give up the control over the content, and the frequency of information; however, it is essential for marketers to realize that reviews and discussions, as user-generated content, serve to demonstrate a company's transparency. When online retailers like Amazon[7] started inviting individuals (such as consumers and users) to give their opinions, there was no stopping the trend; that is, the communication in present-day has drastically altered into a medium that is composed of millions of people who can actually contribute or detract from a marketing message. Consequently, compared to offline traditional marketing channels

[7] Amazon.com, Inc. is an American international electronic commerce company with headquarters in Seattle, Washington, United States. It is the world's largest online retailer.

(such as television, newspaper, magazines, and so on), word-of-mouth solely relies on social media outlets in this digital age, due to the fact that websites allow users to create their own virtual spaces which fosters and ignite the word-of-mouth.

Conversation in traditional media is one-way: the company spoke, an audience listened. Mass messages are filtered through opinion leaders to the mass audience, in which opinion leader is very hard to be identified since they are not formal experts and do not necessarily provide advice but have a certain degree of influence on consumers (Katz and Lazarsfeld, 1955).

As it is said, social media has put consumers back to the center by enabling them to engage in conversations, and neither the decisions are made by a few individuals nor the message being sent to the masses by the brand owner. Smith and Zook (2011) have pointed out that customers, first, talk to each other (C2C) with the online platforms, and secondly back to the company (C2B). Online communities have bridged the communication gap between brands and consumers, and eventually this certain type of communication flow fosters a web communication between customers and opinion leaders (Smith and Zook, 2011).

Regarding the information processing theory of consumer choice, it is mentioned that there are vast amount of advertisements competing with each other in order to grasp individuals' attention (Fennis and Stroebe, 2011) and the fact that human beings have an obvious limited brain capacity in processing information; therefore, it is a challenge for each discrete message to get heard above the din (extraneous factors that distract or distort the message), even if marketers have the right message (Silverman, 2001).

In relating to social media marketing, the biggest fear of companies and brands is to give up the control over the content, and the frequency of information; however, it is essential for marketers to realize that reviews and discussions, as user-generated contents, serve to demonstrate a company's transparency (Weber, 2007).

In the notion of communication models theories (Goldenberg, Han and Lehmann, 2010), the findings (Katz and Lazarsfeld, 1955; Bulte and Wuyts, 2007) have provided that opinion leaders are those initially exposed to certain media content who interpret the message based on their own opinion, and are more active than others both in seeking information and in conveying it to others. (Wuyts *et al.*, 2010)

According to Lazarsfeld and Katz's hypothesis (1955), the information is channeled to the masses through opinion leaders, who have a more literate understanding of media content, explain and diffuse the content to others. Listeners, in turns, subsequently feed back to the opinion leaders (Smith and Zook, 2011).

"Customers are screaming to be more engaged with the companies that affect their lives," is how Diane Hessan, president and CEO of Communispace[8], describes the change, social media has brought to consumers. She further addresses that "Blooming trends like blogging, online communities, flash mobbing, buzz agents, and social networks show that customers have a lot to say – they want to be asked and they want to be involved" (Communispace, 2013).

Smith and Zook (2011) have pointed out that customers, first, talk to each other (C2C) with the online platforms and secondly back to the company (C2B). Online communities have bridged the communication gap between brands and consumers, and eventually this certain type of communication flow fosters a web communication between customers and opinion leaders which spins around the brand (Smith and Zook, 2011).

1.4 Social Networking Sites- Company Perspective

Social networks are used as a marketing tool for many different purposes. Companies use these sites to gain information on their target market, and how people feel about their products. They can also use these sites to gain information on their competition. Small businesses may also use these sites to promote their brand.

These networks allow thousands of people to network with each other, meeting new people that may benefit their business or services being offered. Networking with different people through these sites is an excellent way to create new contacts, and potentially create new customers or business associates.

---

[8] A registered company working as a provider of web-based software and services that help companies leverage the power of online communities.

The most valuable part of marketing using social networks is that it allows people to market their services to a large market at no cost. Thousands of people enter these sites daily. Therefore they are able to reach a mass market free of charge.

The popular network Facebook offers a free classifieds section where people are able to post things such as job listings, items for sale, or services available. Companies of all sorts are able to place advertisements for their products or services, as well as post job opportunities. People are also able to market themselves by listing their skills and abilities for employers to view.
Another popular social network, MySpace, is widely used by its members as a way of promoting themselves. Many musicians or actors wishing to gain some free recognition will place videos and songs on their pages for others to view. This site also allows members to send their videos to other members, and gain more recognition and feedback.

One large benefit to marketing on social networks is the pass along factor. Users of these networks tend to pass along items that are of interest to them, or that they believe their friends will find interesting. Members are also able to pass along their own postings to other site members, whether they know them or not.

Social networks are also beneficial to companies who are wishing to create e-mail lists to send coupons or advertisements through the mail. Companies may post bulletins on websites encouraging people to sign up for their daily newsletters, etc. In doing this many companies are able to greatly increase their mailing lists.

Placing paid advertisements, such as banners, on these sites can also benefit a company greatly based on the amount of hits the sites receive each day. Thousands of members view these pages daily which means ads placed on these sites will reach a mass audience.

Marketers are also able to monitor social networking sites, to read up on how people are viewing their brands. These sites allow them to see what their competitors are doing, and how customers view the competition. Receiving this feedback from customers allows marketers to understand what the target market is looking for, what people like about their products or services, and what needs to be improved.

Social networks also allow marketers to gain information on their potential customers. By viewing user profiles, marketers are able to gather information regarding the demographics and psychographics of potential customers, making them better able to identify those that fit into their target market. This information can often be time consuming and costly. Having social networks to help them find this information is quite beneficial to marketers. Many of the social networking sites allow users to create groups regarding specific topics. This makes it much easier for marketers to find much of the information regarding their target market, and their competitors.

Social networks are a very valuable marketing tool. With the recent growth in popularity of many of the networking websites, marketers are better able to market their brands to a mass market without having to invest the time and money that they would by marketing through other means. These sites are beneficial to companies both big and small, and allow companies to market themselves in new and creative ways.

The most valuable part of marketing using social networks is that it allows people to market their services to a large market at no cost. Thousands of people enter these sites daily. Therefore they are able to reach a mass market free of charge.

The popular network Facebook offers a free classifieds section where people are able to post things such as job listings, items for sale, or services available. Companies of all sorts are able to place advertisements for their products or services, as well as post job opportunities. People are also able to market themselves by listing their skills and abilities for employers to view.

Another popular social network, MySpace, is widely used by its members as a way of promoting themselves. Many musicians or actors wishing to gain some free recognition will place videos and songs on their pages for others to view. This site also allows members to send their videos to other members, and gain more recognition and feedback.

One large benefit to marketing on social networks is the pass along factor. Users of these networks tend to pass along items that are of interest to them, or that they believe their friends will find interesting. Members are also able to pass along their own postings to other site members, whether they know them or not.

Social networks are also beneficial to companies who are wishing to create e-mail lists to send coupons or advertisements through the mail. Companies may post bulletins on websites encouraging people to sign up for their daily newsletters, etc. In doing this many companies are able to greatly increase their mailing lists.

Placing paid advertisements, such as banners, on these sites can also benefit a company greatly based on the amount of hits the sites receive each day. Thousands of members view these pages daily which means ads placed on these sites will reach a mass audience.

Marketers are also able to monitor social networking sites, to read up on how people are viewing their brands. These sites allow them to see what their competitors are doing, and how customers view the competition. Receiving this feedback from customers allows marketers to understand what the target market is looking for, what people like about their products or services, and what needs to be improved.

Social networks also allow marketers to gain information on their potential customers. By viewing user profiles, marketers are able to gather information regarding the demographics and psychographics of potential customers, making them better able to identify those that fit into their target market. This information can often be time consuming and costly. Having social networks to help them find this information is quite beneficial to marketers. Many of the social networking sites allow users to create groups regarding specific topics. This makes it much easier for marketers to find much of the information regarding their target market, and their competitors.

Social networks are a very valuable marketing tool. With the recent growth in popularity of many of the networking websites, marketers are better able to market their brands to a mass market without having to invest the time and money that they would by marketing through other means. These sites are beneficial to companies both big and small, and allow companies to market themselves in new and creative ways.

According to media reports, Indian organizations use social media much more than the global average and their counterparts in emerging economies. As per a study conducted by consulting firm, Ernst & Young, "Social-Media-Marketing-India-Trends-Study-2013", most social media-savvy organizations in India use this medium to build communities.

Most of the social media-savvy organizations in India use the medium to build communities and advocate usage while 76.1% use social media as a platform to highlight brand news. Around 16% of organizations, which use social media for both the above reasons, also use it for customer service, lead generation, and research indicating high social maturity and moving toward getting business meanings out of engagements.
Facebook is the most important platform for marketers in India for engaging customers, followed by Twitter, YouTube and blogging.

Many social media-savvy organizations are already using emerging platforms such as Pinterest, Google Plus, and Foursquare. More than half of the social media-savvy organizations surveyed regularly engage with bloggers or online influencers who have authority and strong following.
Social media-savvy organizations in India have conducted campaigns where social media is the leading component. Among the respondents, 87.5% said they have conducted campaigns where social media was the leading component. More than half of the surveyed organizations have speeded up processes or have shown a special favour for their online fans and followers that they wouldn't normally do for their offline customers.

A majority of social media savvy organizations prefer to post generic updates instead of brand updates. Social media-savvy organizations post multiple updates a day.
Majority of social media-savvy organizations respond to fan queries within 30 to 60 minutes on Twitter and within 30 minutes to a few hours on Facebook. Picture contests are the most popular contests among social media-savvy organizations in India — most contests are organized monthly.

Majority of social media-savvy organizations in India surveyed had social media guidelines for better governance and online monitoring programs to listen to conversations; however, less than half have crisis manuals. Many social media-savvy organizations in India use tools for online monitoring, response management, or managing social media platforms. A couple of social media-savvy organizations in India have conducted research using social media tools to get customer feedback and understand more about customer behavior. Many media-savvy organizations in India have created mobile phone apps and one-fourth plans to create one.

Majority of social media-savvy organizations use social media ads to promote online campaigns and brand awareness, and find them beneficial. 83% of the social media-savvy organizations surveyed said that they have used social media ads, with majority of the ads being used to promote a contest/promotion or for brand awareness. 88.6% said they find social media ads to be beneficial in achieving those objectives.

Majority of social media savvy organizations in India measure social media efforts through platform-specific parameters. 81% of the social media savvy organizations surveyed said that they measure their social media efforts through platform-specific parameters such as likes, people talking about this, etc. 46.7% of the organizations surveyed said they have not measured revenue from their social media efforts. On the positive side, some organizations are already measuring social media efforts through leads, sentiment, brand visibility and have seen increase in revenue from social media efforts.

Almost half of the social media-savvy organizations spend 1%–5% of their marketing budget on social media, most social media budgets are below INR10 million. 41.5% of social media-savvy organizations said that around 1%–5% of their marketing budget in spent on social media. Three-fourths of the organizations surveyed have their social media budget below INR 10 million, while a little above a quarter of the organizations surveyed have social media budgets exceeding INR 20 million.

Majority of social media efforts in India are managed by marketing teams. 76.7% of social media-savvy organizations said they have their marketing department handling social media with the rest being handled by a cross functional team/across functions or by the PR/communications team. Other than marketing, 34.6% said they use social media for thought leadership and 26.9% said they use social media for CSR (corporate social responsibility). A majority (70.2%) said they have an in house social media expert in middle management.

Majority of social media-savvy organizations in India use standalone digital agencies as compared to PR or ad agencies. 73.8% of surveyed social media-savvy organizations have chosen standalone digital agencies as compared to PR, ad agencies, or freelancers. 59.1% of the organizations surveyed also said that they are happy with their current agencies while 40.9% responded with either a "maybe" or a "no."*(Source of above data: Ernst & Young, "Social-Media-Marketing-India-Trends-Study-2013")*

Social media-savvy organizations are very optimistic about the role of social media in their organizations. Though measures such as sales and leads are not very evident for all organizations, they have realized that it plays an important role in generating insights and engaging with customers on a continued basis. Social media has helped organizations to create their own communities of fans, customers or prospects. In the future, organizations hope to focus more on social media and are looking forward to greater adoption within their organizations.

The above mentioned study was conducted in social media savvy organizations. But implementation of social networks in marketing communication is still at a nascent stage in many organizations.

1.5 Need for a Study on the Opportunities and Challenges of Social Networking Sites in India

Social networking sites are still in their growing stage in developing economies like India. Facebook, the most prominent site has 114 million active users at the end of June 2014 (Source: Forbes), only behind United States. India has a huge population of youth who are tech savvy, and gradually becoming upwardly mobile. In India, Facebook remains the social media of choice. Facebook has grown at light speed in India. In 2010, there were only 8 million Facebook active users in India. According to Facebook Company Statistics, 84% of India's Facebook users assess the site from their smart phones. Mobile social networking has become significant.

Social networking sites provide ample opportunities to the marketers to reach out customers.

Facebook is working with marketers in India to help businesses understand the word-of-mouth advertising and power of social media. The company's billion dollar acquisitions, first of Instagram and most recently of true text app, "Whats App", keep the company relevant even if its original business is starting to contract.

It is important for the marketers to understand how electronic word of mouth can be used in marketing communication. The opportunities for marketers lie in gaining valuable information from electronic word of mouth in social networks, which can establish and strengthen their long term relationships with consumers. A study into consumers' perception towards social networking sites would give the required insight to understand the habits and usage of social networks. An empirical study is required to study the impact of social relationship variables on electronic word of mouth communication.

Many organizations have integrated social media in their marketing communication programme. This new platform has opened up enormous opportunities and unique way to reach right target audience. It becomes important to analyze the purposes of usage of social networks and metrics of evaluation of their effectiveness.

Privacy and safety issues become a major challenge in the use of social networks. Moreover, calculating the return on investment or measuring key performance indicators, become very important. These issues have to be explored to get a holistic view of the effectiveness and impact of social networks.

1.6 Outline of the Thesis

The thesis is organized into 8 chapters. Chapter 1 introduces the topic of the present research. This chapter offers background information related to social networking sites and use of social networking sites in context of consumers and companies. In Chapter 2, existing literature has been reviewed, and a conceptual framework of consumer study has been designed. Also, a framework of the study with companies' perspective is being discussed. This is followed by Chapter 3 on Research Methodology, which describes the method for the empirical investigation. The hypotheses guiding the consumers' and companies' study and theoretical discussion of the rationale for them are also outlined in Chapter 3. Next, Chapter 4 delineates data analysis and interpretation. Challenges and opportunities for social networking sites in India are summarized in Chapter 5. Discussion and conclusion is summarized in chapter 6. Recommendations and implications of the research are provided in Chapter 7. Limitations and directions of future research related to studies are addressed in Chapter 8. After the final chapter, a list of reference is given, which is followed by appendices.

A detailed study of the relevant literature is given in the ensuing chapter.

The chapter will also present the development of the conceptual framework for the study of attitude of Indian consumers towards social networks. The chapter will discuss how electronic word of mouth is significant in changing consumer behavior. Chapter 2 also includes the conceptual framework of study related to usage of social networks for marketing purpose, and identifying the key performance indicators of social network platforms, within different organizations.

Chapter 2

Literature Review

Literature Review

Chapter Overview

The aim of this chapter is to provide a review of the extant literature available in the form of company reports and in relevant databases like Emerald, EBSCO and Pro Quest, Science Direct, JSTOR, etc. This chapter presents an in-depth study of consumer engagement in social networking sites. The chapter also elaborates on the use of social networks in marketing communication across Indian organizations.

This chapter is divided into two parts. The first one is about establishing determinants of consumer engagement in social networking sites. This part discusses consumer behavior in social networks, word of mouth communication, social relationships in social networks and the need to study drivers of electronic word of mouth in social networking sites.

The second part of the chapter discusses the integration of social networking sites in marketing communication programs implemented by brands and marketing organizations.

Consumer Perspective

2.1 Consumer Behavior in Online Social Networks

One of the most challenging areas for researchers and companies is consumer behavior. There are different studies analyzing consumer behavior or factors implementing online purchasing behavior.

Engel, Kollat and Blackwell (1973) proposed that consumer decision process is widely recognized by scholars and consists of five stages – need recognition, information search, evaluation, purchase, and post-purchase. At each stage, social media can create a significant opportunity.

The table 2.1 below mentions social media opportunities and enabling services along with each stage of consumer decision making process.

Table 2.1: Consumer Buying Process and Social Media Opportunities

Stage	Social Media Opportunities	Enabling Services
Need Recognition	Create and raise Awareness	Connecting and sharing with friends, spending more time and identifying
Information Search	Provide context	Bookmarking, information sharing, personalized pages services
Evaluation	Build trust	Opportunities to provide feedback and reviews
Purchase	Transaction	Transactional (group buying, buy for friends, etc.) services
Post-purchase	Increase satisfaction	Supporting and personalized services

(Adapted From Gartner, 2010, and Davidaviciene, Gatautis, 2010)

J.Owyang (2012) also agrees on proposed consumer journey approach, but tends to consider this journey dynamic due to 3 factors:

- Recent development and advances in technologies' deployment
- Change of medium
- Increasing power of word of mouth

The dynamic nature of consumer journey appears due to the empowerment of consumers through technologies which leads to faster, smarter and more informed decisions. This enables consumers' access to real time information, to get information from their friends as well as share information with friends.

J.Owyang (2010) proposed engagement in online social networking sites framework which was constructed after analyzing companies' activities in social networking sites (Table 2.2).

J.Owyang and C.Lee (2010) even proposed new segmentation approach – social graphic. According to them "companies should first understand how their customers use social technologies before they choose the tools. Social graphics measure how customers use social technologies, where they are online, and how it influences them in the context of the customer lifecycle.

The proposed approach is similar to classical approach for user segmentation striving to answer key questions (Owyang, Lee 2010):

Where are your customers online?

What are your customers' social behaviors online?

What social information or people do your customers rely on?

What is your customers' social influence?

How do customers use social in context of your products?

Table 2.2 - Consumer Engagement Process in Online Social Networking Sites

Stage	**Description**
Watching	Seeking social-created content to help with making decisions, learning from peers, or entertainment
Sharing	Want to share the information they have with peers, both to support others, and demonstrate knowledge
Commenting	Actively participate, support, or contribute ideas/opinions, but usually one-off's
Producing	Want to express identity, own content, be heard, or be recognized
Curating	Invested in success of a product, service, or community, want to give back, or be recognized

(Adapted from J.Owyang and Ch. Lee, 2010)

J.Owyang and Ch. Lee (2010) proposed approach demonstrates attempt to connect behavioral process and users typology.

Technology use and adoption theory reflecting Rogers's innovation diffusion model explains how technology is deployed by different type of users and defines five categories of users: *Innovators, Early Adopters, Early Majority, Late Majority, Laggards.*

The wide adoption of this theory might be also explained by high degree of generalization. The proposed categorization considers the use of technologies (in this case use of social networking sites) and time of adoption is differentiating factor. But such category doesn't reflect how really social networking sites are used (how actually consumers behave).

Valck, van Bruggen and Wierenga (2009) after analysis of virtual communities' members' behavior identified 6 behavior/user types (Table 2.3).

Table 2.3: Social Networking Sites Users' Typology

Type	Description
Core Members	Users make extensive use of the community's knowledge reservoir by retrieving information. At the same time, they are frequent suppliers to this knowledge reservoir by submitting recipes, articles, and reviews. Furthermore, they participate actively in forum discussions and chat sessions.
Conversationalists	Users retrieve and supply information, but not to such a high extent as the core members. It is especially their relative high level of engagement in forum discussions and chat sessions that characterizes their participation pattern.
Informationalists	Users visit frequency and duration is comparable to that of the conversationalists. They tend to visit the community somewhat less frequent, but they spend more time per visit. Users show reciprocity in their behavior by also supplying information to the community, although they do this to a lesser extent compared with the core members.
Hobbyists	Users are the community's most frequent visitors with long duration visits, i.e., they visit the community almost daily for about one hour. Users' online activities are not primarily focused on the retrieval, supply, or discussion of information. Instead, they are engaged in updating and maintaining their personal page within the community and in writing guest book messages; activities that usually involve playing around with techniques such as uploading music, pictures, illustrations, and cartoons.
Functionalists	The respondents in this cluster visit the community approximately once a week for about 15 min.
Opportunists	They are the community's least frequent visitors and their visits usually do not last long, i.e., they visit the community on average less than once a week for no more than 15 min. While they are online, they are mainly engaged in retrieving information in the form of recipes, not articles or reviews. They hardly supply any information, nor do they join forum discussions and chat sessions.

Source: (Valck, van Bruggen and Wierenga, 2009)

Another approach was proposed by Brandtzaeg and Heim (2011), categorizing users by two criteria – how active are users (low activity-high activity) and what is the purpose of using social networking sites (informational or recreational). This approach created 5 categories.

Sporadics: The 'sporadics' are so named because they visit the community only from time to time, but not on a frequent basis. These users have a low level of participation and tend more toward an informational mode since they, for the most part, check their status and see if somebody has contacted them.

Lurkers: Lurkers make up the largest user category. They are named 'lurkers' since they are quite low in participation and participate in activities that are more related to recreation. These users are somewhat involved in several activities, but only passively or to a small degree. In addition to "see if somebody has tried to contact me", lurkers score high on "kill some time".

Socializers: Their behavior is characterized by recreational in terms of 'small talk' with others, but the users' participation level is high. They score high on 'write letters and or messages', 'contact others', and 'look for a new friend'.

Debaters: Debaters are as high as socializers in terms of participation level, characterized by being highly involved in discussions, reading, and writing contributions in general. In addition, this participation mode is related to a more informal practice.

Actives: 'Actives' are so labeled because these users are engaged in almost all kinds of participation activities within the community, which includes being a member to "publish and share pictures".

The results of previous studies imply that the information exchange via word of mouth activities has important implications on the consumer behavior, and therefore is up most important within marketing research.

The next section will discuss word of mouth (word of mouth) communication in detail, and the importance of electronic word of mouth in marketing communication process.

2.2 Word of Mouth Communication: An Overview

Word of Mouth in general, is referred as an informal form of communication between people about products and services (Dichter, 1966; Westbrook, 1987; Singh 1988; East, Hammond & Wright, 2007). Arndt (1967) added that word of mouth occurs in form of an oral face-to-face communication. Mullen and Johnson (1990) distinguished word of mouth from advertising by adding that word of mouth is an "unpaid and unsponsored" form of communication. Therefore, word of mouth can be defined as an unsponsored face-to-face interaction between a "sender" and a "receiver" regarding services and products.

One of the first studies specifically about word of mouth was conducted by Katz and Lazarsfeld (1955) where they found out that word of mouth is seen as the most important source of information for household items. Furthermore, Arndt (1967) added that in terms of high perceived risk, a person is even more likely to be influenced by word of mouth. Scholars contribute findings across many different products (Engel, Kegerreis & Blackwell, 1969), and furthermore, distinguished between positive and negative word of mouth (Arndt, 1967; Rogers, 1962; Richins, 1983). To date, there is still mixed evidence, regarding the prevalence of positive versus negative word of mouth (Angelis, *et al.,* 2012).

On the one hand, findings showed that consumers are more likely to share negative word of mouth, as a result of their dissatisfaction of a product or service and moreover to prevent others from buying (Heskett, Sasser & Schlesinger, 1997; Kamins, Folkes & Pernes, 1997, Anderson, 1998). Other studies showed the opposite e.g. consumers are more likely to share positive word of mouth, as an outcome of involvement, self-enhancement or dissonance reduction (Engel, Blackwell & Miniard, 1993; Hennig-Thurau *et al.,* 2004; Keller, 2007). However Lutz (1975) and Anderson (1998) stated that negative word of mouth has a greater impact on consumer behavior than positive word of mouth.

In other studies (King & Summers, 1970; Granovetter, 1973; Brown & Reingen, 1987; Rogers, 1993), marketing scholarship focused on different characteristics like the importance of influential consumers (opinion leaders) and the impact of social structures. The results of previous studies imply that the information exchange via word of mouth activities has important implications on the consumer behavior, and therefore is up most important within marketing research. However, existing literature has proved that social structure has an influence on word of mouth communication as well e.g. "word of mouth's impact depends on who is talking to whom" (Godes & Mayzlin, 2004).

Granovetter (1973) defined relationships between a sender and a receiver of word of mouth communication as being "strong" or "weak". Those relationships or "ties" are based on frequency of contact and social relation. In the area of sociology, Granovetter (1973) argues that in terms of information diffusion "weak ties" are more important as they are connected through different social networks; however, they are less influential. "Strong ties" are much more important in terms of word of mouth influence. Strong ties are well connected with each other as a result of similar interests, social structures, etc. Therefore the opinion of one of those ties is seen as much more credible (Brown & Reingen, 1987). Furthermore, Duhan *et al.*, (1997) stated that weak-tie sources are mainly utilized when the consumer already has previous knowledge and only need a confirmation of his opinion.

In contradiction, "Consumers who perceive great difficulty in the decision tasks are likely to look toward strong-tie sources for recommendations" (Duhan *et al.*, 1997). Reingen *et al.*, (1984) investigated the role of influential consumers in terms of brand preferences within sorority houses[1] and found out that those who lived together have more common brand preferences than those who lived alone. Therefore, it can be assumed that influential consumers (opinion leaders) within social structures are important as well (Godes & Mayzlin, 2004).

Studies (Katz & Lazarsfeld, 1955; King & Summers, 1970; Jacoby & Hoyer, 1981; Bloch & Richins, 1983; Rogers, 1993) have confirmed the statement, that there are consumers within communities who are seen as more respected, credible, and influential than others which are commonly referred to as opinion leaders. Those can be identified as 1) being involved in more social activities than others, 2) spending more time on a specific product than others and 3) they are more enthusiastic about sharing their experience about a product (Wu & Yang, 2010). Research has directed in identifying the key characteristics of those influential consumers (King & Summers, 1970; Robertson, 1971). Feick and Price (1987) stated that product involvement can be one explanation for an opinion leader to talk

[1] Sorority housing refers largely to the houses or housing areas in which fraternity members live and work together. These houses also serve to host social gatherings, meetings, and functions that benefit the community.

about products or services. Rogers (1995) noted that opinion leaders can lose their credibility when they adopt new ideas too quickly. He argues that the role of an opinion leader is to reduce uncertainty about a new product; therefore, he should send out a well-thought decision.

However, the nature of word of mouth communication and the impact of social structure and opinion leaders underlies its spontaneous manner (Stern, 1994), which is hard to control and moreover, hard to measure as a result of the oral transmission via face to face.

The significance of information consumers obtain from interpersonal sources in influencing consumer decision making has been well recognized in marketing and consumer behavior literature (Engel, Blackwell, and Kegerreis, 1969; Gilly *et al.,* 1998; Goldsmith and Clark 2008; Wiedmann, Hennigs, and Langner, 2007).

Although non-personal or commercial messages such as advertising may be important in developing consumer awareness and initial interest in products or services, word-of-mouth, defined as the act of exchanging marketing information among consumers, has been found to play a more essential role in changing consumer attitude and behavior related to products and services (Engel, Blackwell, and Kegerreis, 1969; Gilly *et al.,* 1998; Grewal, Cline, and Davies, 2003; Katz and Lazarsfeld, 1955; Rogers, 1995). For example, studies suggest that word of mouth influences the speed and rate of innovation diffusion (Mahajan, Muller, and Srivastava, 1990; Rogers, 1995) and is imperative to the flow of information in social networks for product adoption (Frenzen and Nakamoto, 1993).

In addition, because interpersonal sources in general are seen as more credible than non-personal or commercial sources (Feick and Price, 1987), consumers often rely on informal word of mouth when they seek information for their purchases (Goldsmith and Clark, 2008). As a result, generating positive word of mouth in consumers' social networks has become a crucial technique for marketers to build and maintain strong brand relationships with highly engaged consumers (Smith *et al.,* 2007).

In recent years, the advance and evolution of new media technologies such as the Internet has increased consumer opportunities to not only interact with members of their pre-existing social network but also make and communicate with new friends online (Hung and Li, 2007; Niederhoffer *et al.,* 2007). With the rapid development of the Internet, word of mouth has taken a significant turn and evolved to electronic word-of-mouth.

Electronic word-of-mouth refers to a particular type of word of mouth which occurs in the online setting (Dwyer, 2007) and can be observed in many different online channels, such as discussion forums, product reviews, and emails. Several researchers have examined the influence of Internet-based electronic word of mouth on product success (Chevalier and Mayzlin, 2006), virtual consumer community (Hung and Li, 2007), and explored how the electronic word of mouth process influences consumers' online behaviors (De Bruyn and Lilien, 2008). While current research has focused on the outcomes of electronic word of mouth (e.g., sales), little is known about the drivers of electronic word of mouth or factors influencing consumers' word of mouth behavior in computer-mediated environments, particularly in social networking sites, an emerging user-generated social medium.

Social networking sites have been paid mounting attention from scholars and marketers. Social networking sites attract a fast-growing number of consumers by enabling them to visualize and articulate their social network and engage in social interactions in a dynamic, interactive, multi-modal form over the Internet (Boyd and Ellison, 2007). Social networking sites are of paramount importance to electronic word of mouth as consumers freely share their experience and opinions and rapidly spread information and opinions regarding products and services in their social networks comprised of friends, personal contacts, and other acquaintances (Raacke and Bonds-Raacke, 2008).

No wonder marketers currently invest considerable resources in encouraging positive electronic word of mouth in the social venue by setting up their brand profile pages (i.e., brand communities) and engaging consumers to make friends with the brand (Morrissey, 2007). Despite the huge potential of social networking sites for engendering and facilitating electronic word of mouth, research on why and how electronic word of mouth emerges in the emerging online social environment remains scant.

Given that relationship building is the primary objective of social networking site users, a question arises as to what social factors influence consumers' engagement in electronic word of mouth in this online hangout place. Although a few studies provide initial insights into the drivers of consumer electronic word of mouth behavior in computer-mediated environments (Balasubramanian and Mahajan, 2001; Hennig-Thurau *et al.,* 2004), our theoretical knowledge of consumer behavior in the emerging social media, social networking sites is limited. Empirical investigation is timely and necessary to enhance our understanding of the determinants of electronic word of mouth in social networking sites, the seemingly universal phenomenon.

In the last few years, with the enormous growth of the internet, brand choices and personal influences (word of mouth) are increasingly taking place in computer mediated environments (Kozinets, 2002). This offers two major modifications within the traditional word of mouth research strand: 1) word of mouth can be investigated easier and more time efficient, as this kind of word of mouth is transferred in written form instead of oral face-to-face communication, and 2) word of mouth itself is changing as well within online environments which are at this stage called electronic word of mouth.

Scholars have investigated many different factors within the traditional word of mouth literature. However, analyzing offline word of mouth behavior is very limited as well as difficult (Godes & Mayzlin, 2004). Within computer mediated environment, the content is in written format which makes it easier to capture information of word of mouth communication (Huang, *et al.,* 2011). Furthermore, Dellarocas (2003) stated that "The Internet allows this powerful social force to be precisely measured and controlled through proper engineering of information systems". Electronic word of mouth marketing is an important feature on the internet as it provides many different channels for consumers to share their experiences and exchange information (Trusov, Bucklin & Pauwels, 2009).

Kozinets (1998) was one of the first scholars who investigated communications within computer mediated environments by describing the formation of different communities where consumers are now able to meet up in a location independent environment. Years later, with the rapid growth of the internet, "traditional word-of-mouth has been extended to electronic media, such as online discussion forums, electronic bulletin board systems, newsgroups, blogs, review sites, and social networking sites" (Cheung & Lee, 2012).

"One of the fastest-growing arenas of the World Wide Web is the space of so-called social networking sites" (Trusov, Bucklin & Pauwels, 2009). Social networking platforms such as Facebook, Twitter and LinkedIn, to name a few have attracted millions of users; many of them are using those platforms every day and are expanding at an enormously fast rate (Qualman, 2009).

Social networking sites can be defined as computer mediated services which allow users to (1) maintain and build networks of friends for social or professional purposes, (2) to construct personal user profiles and newsfeeds, where they (3) share information to their network (Boyd & Ellison, 2007, Trusov, Bucklin & Pauwels, 2009). The Contacts within Social Networking Sites are in general members of their social networking sites which are seen as more credible and trustworthy (Chu & Choi, 2011). Furthermore, Robert, Dennis & Ahuj (2008) added that a social relationship is the prime factor in terms of trust and credibility.

Word of mouth marketing is the oldest but the most effective marketing tool. With social networking sites, the impact of word of mouth marketing is greatly amplified. Every customer has the ability to market a brand to hundreds and even thousands of friends within a matter of seconds. Social media is modern day word of mouth marketing. It is about how businesses today interact and build strong relationships with their individual customers on social networks.

2.2.1 Characteristics of Different Kinds of Word of Mouth

To comply with the different characteristics within the computer mediated environment as well as the characteristics within social networking sites, Hoffman & Novak (1996) and later Huang *et al.,* (2011) adapted the traditional communication model which can be, within the research strand of electronic word of mouth, classified into two stages: 1) One-to-one networks / One-to-many communication which represents electronic word of mouth basically within social networking sites or 2) Many-to-many communication which are in terms of electronic word of mouth mainly recommendation systems or discussion forums.

Table 2.4: Offline Word of Mouth vs. Online Word of Mouth

	Offline Word of Mouth	Online Word of Mouth	
Medium	Talk, telephone, personal meeting	Social networking sites	Discussion forums, Blogs
Form	Oral	Written	Written
Synchronicity	Synchronous	Asynchronous or synchronous	Asynchronous or Synchronous
Type of interaction	Face-to-face	Virtual interaction	Virtual interaction
Format	Linear communication	Linear or non-linear communication	Non-linear Communication
Relationship between sender and receiver	Real social ties	Mostly real social ties or virtual ties	Mostly anonymous or virtual ties
Ease of Transmission	Difficult to transmit	Easy to transmit or Forward	Easy to transmit or forward

Adapted from: Hoffmann and Novak (1996) and Huang *et al.* (2011)

One-to-one/many communication is the appropriate communication model for electronic word of mouth with social networking sites. Social networking sites can be distanced from online forums or blogs as they differ in other ways as well. A social networking site offers users the possibility to disclose information about themselves as they sign in with their real name. Therefore the person and the person's characteristics and attributes are in focus. In existing literature, social networking sites are often referred as a person's extended offline social network. This means that people use these sites to communicate with people they already know about things they have in common.

Prior research has examined different psychological motives within electronic word of mouth as well as traditional word of mouth. Some scholars argue that positive electronic word of mouth/word of mouth is driven by a desire to help a brand (Sundaram, Mitra and Webster, 1998) or product involvement (Dichter, 1966).

Another factor was the selfless concern to the welfare of others (Sundaram, Mitra & Webster, 1998). Furthermore, Wojnicki and Godes (2011) argued that there is a desire to signal expertise to others. One of the most prevalent needs that can drive the transmission is self-enhancement (Fiske, 2001; Angelis, *et al.,* 2012). Self enhancement is a desire to improve a positive self-image, maintain self-esteem and improve the self-concept (Brown, Collins, and Schmidt, 1988). This psychological desire is even more critical in context of social structures (traditional word of mouth) (Smith, 1968).

Berger & Heath (2007) found out that people share content which signals their social identity e.g. they establish an identity and therefore choose products which confirm this identity, which is called "the standard fashion cycle (Hebdige, 1987; Simmel, 1971). However, the stated psychological drivers are more likely within word of mouth as in electronic word of mouth (Wojnicki & Godes, 2011; Hennig-Thurau, *et al.*, 2004).

The key differences between electronic word of mouth within recommendation forums or blogs to electronic word of mouth within social networking sites is that 1) People are not anonymous anymore 2) Users can add other users to their networks by defining them as "friends" (hereafter contacts). Within social networking sites, users maintain different levels of privacy in terms of what information (including electronic word of mouth) can be exposed.

In comparison to electronic word of mouth within blogs or other platforms, a sender cannot target their audience; they are publishing it with the purpose to be public. In contradiction, within social networking sites, users or senders of electronic word of mouth know who they are talking to, which refers more to traditional word of mouth as to electronic word of mouth (Impact of social structure, impact of opinion leaders, etc. as mentioned above). 3) Previous research suggests that social networking platforms are mainly used to bring offline social networking sites in an online environment (Boyd & Ellison, 2007).

Furthermore, Ellison, Steinfeld & Lampe (2007) noted that these platforms are more used to maintain relationships, than meeting new people. Therefore, the nature of electronic word of mouth within social networking sites is more similar to traditional word of mouth. Furthermore, Subramani & Rajagopalan (2003) added that there is a lack of analysis of electronic word of mouth behavior within social networking sites, Webster and Morrison (2003) stated that there are only a few studies which have investigated word of mouth in terms of social networking sites.

When people first flocked to social networking sites, the ability to traverse one's own connections and those of others was a critical and defining component of social networking sites. Yet, as profiles faded, media streams emerged and Friends' lists have become more infrastructural; traversing connections has lost its salience as the core participation activity. The ability to see—and traverse—others' contact lists was innovative and important in several ways. From an adoption perspective it enabled users to find shared contacts easily, thus lowering the barriers to initiating contact with other users and enabling users to harness network effects more easily. From a social perspective, it allowed people to easily see the relationships between others, to reconnect with old friends and acquaintances, and to travel through the network in a way that enhanced social interactions.

The next section will explain connect between social relationships and electronic word of mouth behavior in social networking sites.

2.3 Social Relationships in Social Networking Sites

Given the unique social nature of communications in social networking sites, understanding the potential influence of social relationships developed in these sites on brand communications could advance our knowledge of the underlying process of electronic word of mouth. Indeed, a few studies have applied concepts pertaining to social relationships to understand traditional word of mouth referral behavior in offline environments (Brown and Reingen, 1987; Gilly *et al.,* 1998; Reingen and Kernan, 1986). Social capital is one of the concepts that have been frequently discussed in the word of mouth literature. For example, Stephen and Lehmann (2008) suggest that social capital plays an important role in the process of word of mouth transmission. They found that word of mouth transmission fulfills various needs (i.e., validating information, maintaining existing relationships and building new relationships) through transmitters' use of existing social capital or attempt to build new social capital.

Tie strength is another related but conceptually distinct construct. Brown and Reingen (1987) examined the effect of tie strength on the referral flows. Overall, they found that weak ties displayed an important bridging function in facilitating word of mouth referral flows whereas strong ties were perceived as influential in consumers' decision making.

Similarly, Rogers' (1995) study on innovation communications supports that weak ties play a crucial role in disseminating word of mouth information on the aggregate level.

Another dimension of social relationships that is directly relevant to word of mouth is homophily. Studies found that information exchange most frequently occurs between a source and a receiver who are alike, that is, homophilous (Gilly *et al.,* 1998; Lazarsfeld and Merton, 1954; Rogers and Bhowmik, 1970). In the word of mouth context, consumers with a higher level of perceived homophily may be more likely to exchange marketing information when making product choices. Along a similar line, trust, another important factor of social relationships (Chow and Chan, 2008; Fukuyama, 1995), has been found to facilitate the exchange and use of information due to the increased perceived credibility of information when the partner as an information source is trusted in a social relationship (Robert, Dennis, and Ahuja, 2008). As a result, it is reasonable to believe that trust in personal source could also affect the nature and pattern of word of mouth behavior.

Bearden, Netemeyer, and Teel's (1989) consumer susceptibility to interpersonal influence is another variable that is useful to explain the effect of social relationships on consumer reliance on social networking sites as a source of product-focused information. The body of literature on interpersonal communication and word of mouth suggests that consumers with certain personal and personality traits are more likely to disseminate word of mouth to fellow consumers (Feick and Price, 1987; Gilly *et al.,* 1998; Lazarsfeld, Berelson, and Gaudet, 1944).

Consumers with different levels of susceptibility to interpersonal influence might display different patterns of electronic word of mouth communications in social networking sites. For example, consumers with a higher level of susceptibility to interpersonal influence are more likely to engage in peer recommendations than those who are less subject to interpersonal influence. Such behaviors may be reflected in electronic word of mouth behaviors in online social networking sites where information exchange is largely influenced by individual's perceptions of other people.

Therefore, a careful investigation of how interpersonal influence lead to electronic word of mouth is deemed as timely for our understanding of the prevailing phenomenon, product-focused electronic word of mouth in social networking sites and the roles of social relationships in communications online. Collectively, given that social connectivity and relationships are at the core of social networking sites (Choi *et al.*, 2008), these social relationship related factors including social capital, tie strength, homophily, trust, and interpersonal influence serve as the main variables in examining drivers of consumer product-related electronic word of mouth behaviors in social networking sites.

The interconnectivity of the Internet has undergone remarkable growth in recent years and has increased opportunities for consumers to connect with each other (e.g., through online chat rooms and Instant Messaging) in new and flexible ways (Goldsmith and Horowitz, 2006). While traditional media have fragmented into targeting specific demographic segments, the Internet, with its freedom from censorship, low distribution costs, global reach and coverage, and interactivity, enjoys growing popularity. While previous research on Internet-based electronic word of mouth has examined consumer-opinion platforms (Hennig-Thurau *et al.*, 2004), emails (Phelps *et al.*, 2004), and blogs (Thorson and Rodgers, 2006), empirical research on the electronic word of mouth phenomenon in social networking sites is scarce.

Online communication via electronic word of mouth may be most likely to occur extensively and regularly in this emerging social medium. As consumers post their recommendations and opinions about a product or service in their profile pages in social networking sites, they attempt to persuade their friends, acquaintances, or potential consumers to see their point of view and, thus, influence their decision-making.

Given the unique social nature of social networking sites, online social networking sites present an interesting and proper context for examining electronic word of mouth behaviors in computer-mediated environments. In the following section, key, relevant constructs are reviewed to develop the conceptual framework for the present study.

Social relationship is defined as social interactions between two or more individuals. In the context of social networking sites, social relationship variables are particularly important for enhancing the understanding of the underlying electronic word of mouth process as these concepts provide insights into the properties of social relations from which electronic word of mouth behavior arises. Thus, it is imperative to examine whether the influence of social relationships on traditional word of mouth may be applicable to online social networking sites, where social interactions are the major part of users. The following section discusses the meanings and definitions of five social relationship variables that are concerned in this study.

Social Capital

Social capital describes the pattern and intensity of networks among people and the shared values which arise from those networks.

Greater interaction between people generates a greater sense of community spirit.

Definitions of social capital vary, but the main aspects include citizenship, 'neighborliness', social networks and civic participation.

Research has shown that higher levels of social capital are associated with better health, higher educational achievement, better employment outcomes, and lower crime rates.

In other words, those with extensive networks are more likely to be 'housed, healthy, hired and happy'. All of these areas are of concern to both policy-makers and community members alike.

Different types of social capital can be described in terms of different types of networks:

Bonding social capital – describes closer connections between people and is characterized by strong bonds, for example, among family members or among members of the same ethnic group; it is good for 'getting by' in life.

Bridging social capital – describes more distant connections between people and is characterized by weaker, but more cross-cutting ties, for example, with business associates, acquaintances, friends from different ethnic groups, friends of friends, etc; it is good for 'getting ahead' in life

Linking social capital – describes connections with people in positions of power and is characterized by relations between those within a hierarchy where there are differing levels of power; it is good for accessing support from formal institutions. It is different from bonding and bridging in that it is concerned with relations between people who are not on an equal footing.

Social capital is especially applicable to discussing the meanings of social relationships developed and sustained via social networking sites (Choi *et al.,* 2008). Scholars have defined social capital as the set of resources embedded within social networks accessed and used by actors within a network (Coleman, 1988, 1990; Lin, 2001; Putnam, 1993; Robert, Jr., Dennis, and Ahuja, 2008; Scott and Johnson, 2005; Woolcock and Nayaran, 2000). Social capital is not an individual characteristic or a personality trait (Mouw, 2006); instead, it exists in the relationships among people within networks and resources that reside in the networks which are not owned by a single person (Baker, 2000; Chow and Chan, 2008; Mouw, 2006). Accordingly, social capital is essential to community life (Putnam, 1993), personal and business success, and even a satisfying life (Baker, 2000).

The resources of information and ideas from members inherent in networks may affect individual outcomes (Coleman, 1990). As Coleman (1990) suggested, social capital is intangible and is comprised of obligations, shared norms, and expectations that can affect individual behavior and information channels. From a consumer behavior perspective, consumers' reliance on product recommendations and opinions from friends in their personal networks (i.e., reference groups) (Bearden and Etzel, 1982) can be interpreted as evidence of the effect of social capital. Accordingly, social capital may serve as an influential driver that affects consumers' use of social networking sites as a vehicle for electronic word of mouth.

Substantial research has provided evidence that personal communication leads to actual decisions to purchase products and services, whereas advertising increases awareness of them (Coleman, Katz, and Menzel, 1966; Engel, Blackwell, and Kegerreis 1969; Herr, Kardes, and Kim, 1991; Katz and Lazarsfeld, 1955; Price and Feick, 1984). These empirical studies demonstrate the imperative role of social networks in the diffusion or distribution of products and services among consumers. Through social interactions in these personal networks, resources such as information, ideas, norms, emotional support, interpersonal trust, and cooperation, jointly known as social capital, are available to consumers (Baker, 2000; Coleman, 1988).

According to Putnam's (1993) influential work concerning Italian democracy, network qualities, norms of reciprocity, and trust are three elements that compose the basic dimensions of social capital in Italian society. These dimensions have been applied in the later analysis of American society. Other studies have also identified main clusters of social capital based upon its many attributes (Nahapiet and Ghoshal, 1998; Onyx and

Bullen, 2000). For example, Onyx and Bullen (2000) suggest that networks, reciprocity, trust, shared norms, and social agency are five main themes that comprise social capital.

Another important classification developed by Nahapiet and Ghoshal (1998) suggests that social capital contains three dimensions: structural, relational, and cognitive, and each dimension facilitate the creation and share of knowledge. First, the structural dimension associates with social and network relationships, reflecting the potential resource available to an actor and relates to factors that measure the network pattern and density (i.e., tie strength) (Nahapiet and Ghoshal, 1998). Secondly, the relational dimension involves the nature of social relations, such as the level of trust, developed through an interaction among the group members (Nahapiet and Ghoshal, 1998). Lastly, the cognitive dimension refers to shared understanding and interpretations increased through resources. Wasko and Faraj (2005), for instance, suggest that shared culture and goals are important factors. In conclusion, Nahapiet and Ghoshal's (1998) multi-dimensional view of social capital provides valuable implications for examining information management and knowledge integration within social networks (Okoli and Oh, 2007; Robert, Jr., Dennis, and Ahuja, 2008).

In addition to the discussion of dimensions of social capital, two types of social capital have been conceptualized in Putnam's (2000) later study, namely bridging and bonding. Bridging social capital is associated with large, loose networks with fewer "multiplex" relationships, or weak ties that facilitate a wide range of information exchange and resources sharing (Granovetter, 1982; Haythornthwaite, 2000, 2005; Leonard and Onyx, 2003; Naranyan, 1999). Bridging social capital focuses on the capacity to access resources such as information and knowledge from external sources to the community or network (Woolcock and Narayan, 2000). In contrast, bonding social capital involves dense networks or strong ties (Leonard and Onyx, 2003) and is usually derived from kinship networks that provide emotional support or reinforce shared social norms (Naranyan, 1999).

Bridging social capital builds upon reciprocity exchanges created by heterogeneous groups and requires diverse assets and access to information (Pigg and Crank, 2004), whereas bonding social capital is formed through socially homogeneous groups with similar backgrounds, such as similar cultural groups or social characteristics (Flora and Flora, 2004). Further, bridging social capital is associated with a thinner or different sort of trust and is usually purpose-oriented, whereas bonding social capital is related to thick and localized trust that emphasizes emotional charge (Briggs 2003; Pigg and Crank, 2004).

With the development of new communication technologies, researchers in recent years have focused on the likely impact of the Internet on social capital (Best and Krueger, 2006; Kraut *et al.,* 1998; Wellman *et al.,* 1996). Because the development of social capital relies on interactions among people within a network, a question concerning that whether the Internet promotes or impedes offline interpersonal relationships or social interactions has been debated (Best and Krueger, 2006; Kraut *et al.,* 1998). Several researchers argue that the Internet enables the expansion of social networks and increases community social capital by allowing users to join virtual communities and access limitless information (Pigg and Crank, 2004). The relatively lower entry costs of communication increase the capacity to coordinate online and facilitate interpersonal engagement. Thus, the use of the Internet encourages community involvement and civic participation (e.g., Jennings and Zeitner, 2003; Neustadt and Robinson, 2002).

In particular, Williams (2007) found that bridging social capital is more likely to occur than bonding in an online environment due to the easier and faster accessibility (Williams, 2007). The Internet provides freedom from time and space constraints, connecting diverse people from a variety of personal backgrounds, which aids to the formation of bridging social capital. In an online setting, individuals interact with others both within and outside their existing networks easily, allowing them to establish new relationships without emotional support and thereby enhancing bridging social capital while decreasing bonding (Wellman *et al.,* 1996; Williams, 2007).

In regards to social networking sites, current research has found that both bridging and bonding social capital are observed in social networking sites (Choi et al., 2008; Donath, 2007). The unique applications of social networking sites provide consumers with various opportunities to maintain existing personal networks or to expand them, which simultaneously promote bridging and bonding social capital on these sites (Lenhart and Madden, 2007). That is, consumers may not only use social networking sites to maintain close relationships with strong ties (e.g., family and close friends), but also interact with weak ties (e.g., acquaintances and classmates) by engaging in electronic word of mouth communication.

Tie Strength

Drawing on Onyx and Bullen's (2000) discussion of social capital, a social network is one of the important dimensions of social capital and is defined as "a set of individuals ("nodes") and the relationships between them ("ties")" (Stephen and Lehmann, 2008). The resources of social capital such as information can be shared or exchanged through social ties, which vary in terms of their strength (Stephen and Lehmann, 2008). According to Granovetter (1973), tie strength is defined as "the potency of the bond between members of a network" (Mittal, Huppertz, and Khare, 2008). Strong ties such as family and friends form stronger and closer relationships that are within an individual's personal network and are able to provide material and emotional support (Goldenberg, Libai, and Muller, 2001; Pigg and Crank, 2004). Weak ties, on the other hand, are often among weaker and less personal social relationships that are composed of a wide set of acquaintances and colleagues with different cultural and social backgrounds (Goldenberg, Libai, and Muller, 2001; Pigg and Crank, 2004).

Recently, a few studies have found that two types of social capital, bridging and bonding social capital, are both sustained on or via social networking sites (Choi *et al.,* 2008; Donath, 2007). While bridging social capital focuses on the values created by heterogeneous groups and is related to "weak ties," bonding social capital is formed through socially homogeneous groups and is closely associated with "strong ties" (Granovetter, 1982; Haythornthwaite, 2000, 2005). In other words, social networking sites allow consumers to connect with both closer personal contacts such as family members and close friends (strong ties) and less personal contacts that include acquaintances and colleagues (weak ties). These two types of personal contacts may both lead to consumers' electronic word of mouth behavior in social networking sites.

To further enhance the knowledge of the role of social relationships in influencing electronic word of mouth in social networking sites, exploring the relationships between tie strength and electronic word of mouth is needed. According to Granovetter (1973), social ties can be classified as strong and weak ties. Strong ties emphasize the reciprocity nature of social relationships whereas the values of weak ties lie in those loosely connected individuals who give a broader sense of perspectives to others (Pigg and Crank, 2004). Granovetter's (1973) conceptualization of tie strength suggests that the more important, frequent, and durable the tie, the stronger it is.

Operationally, tie strength has also been measured through a variety of variables, such as the importance an individual attaches to the ties, the frequency of social contacts, the intimacy and the reciprocal communications, and the emotional intensity of the ties (Granovetter, 1973; Keister, 1999; Nelson 1989; Weimann, 1983). For example, in Weimann's (1983) study examining the role of conversational ties in the flow of information and influence, the importance attached to the social relation, the frequency of contacts, and the duration of the tie were used to characterize the strength of ties.

Prior research has focused on whether strong or weak ties are the proper structure of social networks for social capital (Burt, 2001; Coleman, 1990; Granovetter, 1983; Li, 2007), indicating that the strength of social ties has important implications for the development of shared resources of social capital (Best and Krueger, 2006). While some argue that strong ties connected in closely-knit personal networks provide the best structure for social capital (Bian, 1997; Coleman, 1990), others view loosely, diverse, generalized networks as preeminent (Burt 2001; Granovetter, 1983). In Granovetter's (1973) seminal work, he proposed the theory of "The Strength of Weak Ties." This offers one of the most valuable theoretical explanations of the process by which face-to-face small group interactions affect inter-group communication phenomena and contribute to the understanding of micro-macro bridge in interpersonal networks. According to Granovetter (1973), tie strength impedes the expansion of the network because as ties strengthen, strongly tied individuals typically tend to possess less-independent social circles with increasing transitivity.

Given this increasing transitivity, individuals are less likely to make new contacts and build new relationships, thereby suggesting that interacting with strong ties hinders the expansion of social capital (Best and Krueger, 2006; Granovetter, 1973).

Conversely, weakly connected pairs tend to possess disparate and wide friendship circles and thus enhance opportunities for individuals to interact at the macro-level and expand their networks (Granovetter, 1973; 1983). With increasing generalized trust, individuals who spend more time with weak ties are more likely to possess greater levels of social capital than those with strong ties whose interactions are usually at the micro-level (Granovetter, 1973, 1983). In sum, Granovetter's (1973) "The Strength of Weak Ties" theory suggests that weak ties serve as an important bridge between groups, thus providing opportunities for individuals to share information and ideas from micro-level behaviors into macro-level patterns (Weimann, 1983).

In the consumer behavior and marketing literature, tie strength has been studied extensively in the research of word of mouth behavior (e.g., Brown and Reingen, 1987; De Bruyn and Lilien, 2008; Frenzen and Nakamoto, 1993; Goldenberg, Libai, and Muller, 2001). These studies have found that both strong and weak ties are the key drivers of information dissemination and have established evidence on the impact of tie strength on word of mouth propagation (Brown and Reingen, 1987; Goldenberg, Libai, and Muller, 2001).

Although advertising and publicity are effective in the early stage of innovations of a new product, strong and weak ties are the main forces propelling product adoption in the growth cycle (Goldenberg, Libai, and Muller, 2001). Consumers' decision-making is often influenced by others with whom they have either random, loose relationships, or by those with whom they have relatively more frequent and intimate interactions in their personal networks (Goldenberg, Libai, and Muller, 2001).

Existing research has examined tie activation in social networks (Brown and Reingen, 1987; De Bruyn and Lilien, 2008; Reingen and Kernan, 1986; Weimann, 1983). For instance, Brown and Reingen (1987) investigated the relationships between social ties and word of mouth referral behavior. Using a network analysis, results from their study suggest that at the macro level, weak ties demonstrated a crucial bridging function, allowing information to disseminate and spread among distinct groups. At the micro level, however, strong ties were more likely to be activated for the flow of referral behavior (Brown and Reingen, 1987).

Furthermore, Weimann (1983) found that weak and strong conversational ties play different roles in the flow of communication. While the spread of information within the group is more likely to occur through strong ties, weak ties are mostly utilized as the bridges between individuals of different groups (Weimann 1983). Weimann (1983) further contends that the "influence" of information mainly arises from strong ties within the group, whereas the bridging function of weak ties is limited to the "flow" of information. In sum, strong ties are more likely to be used and perceived as more influential than weak ties, regardless of the essential role of weak ties in promoting the flow of information and bridging gaps in the broader social system (Brown and Reingen, 1987; Friedkin, 1980; Weimann, 1983).

As more and more companies attempt to influence the spread of electronic word of mouth in social networking sites, marketers need to be aware of the distinctions between strong and weak ties, as both can contribute to electronic word of mouth communications.

Homophily

Another variable which is important in the influence of electronic word of mouth communication in social networking sites is homophily. Homophily refers to the degree to which individuals who interact are congruent or similar on certain attributes, such as demographic variables (Rogers and Bhowmik, 1970), and perceptual similarity of beliefs, values, experience, and lifestyle (Gilly *et al.,* 1998). With frequent and stable interactions, similar individuals have greater access to each other due to propinquity and convenience (Gilly *et al.,* 1998). Because individuals tend to socialize with those who share similar characteristics, often termed social homophily (Mouw, 2006), interpersonal communications are more likely to occur between two individuals who are alike, that is, homophilous (Lazarsfeld and Merton, 1954). As a result, the exchange of information most frequently occurs between a communicator and a receiver who are similar with respect to certain attributes (Rogers and Bhowmik, 1970). In the communication process, both sources and receivers behave based on their perceived characteristics of each other and the message being delivered (Rogers and Bhowmik, 1970).

A receiver's perception of the communication situation, including the degree of similarity, influences the persuasive effect of a message on a receiver's attitude and behavior (Rogers and Bhowmik, 1970). As a homophilous source is more likely to be perceived as credible, trustworthy, and reliable, the effectiveness of communication from a homophilous source may be greater (Rogers and Bhowmik, 1970). For example, although opinion leaders tend to be more competent on the issue being communicated than their followers, opinion leaders often share similar beliefs, norms, and social characteristics with their average follower (Dichter, 1966; Dorothy, 1985; Rogers, 1995; Rogers and Bhowmik, 1970). Thus, opinion leaders are usually viewed as influential members of groups who can exert influence on others' thoughts by swaying opinions with either positive or negative comments (Dorothy, 1985). In the case of social networking sites, consumers may interact with others who are demographically similar or with those quite different, which could influence the nature and extent of electronic word of mouth communications.

In the context of consumer information exchange, as perceived ease of communication increases between similar source and receivers, homophily can facilitate the flow of information in consumers' external searches (Price and Feick, 1984). For example, research has shown that homophilous consumers are more likely to provide personally relevant product information because individuals with similar lifestyles and social characteristics tend to have similar needs and wants in consumption (Feldman and Spencer, 1965). Hence, consumers tend to feel comfortable when interacting with others who are alike in demographic characteristics, such as social status and educational backgrounds (Rogers and Bhowmik, 1970).

Studies have also examined the relationships between homophily and the influence of sources (e.g., Brown and Reingen, 1987; Gilly *et al.,* 1998). These investigations found that consumers are more likely to communicate with similar sources and that the influence of homophilous sources may be greater than heterophilous ones (e.g., expert sources) (Gilly *et al.,* 1998). Feldman and Spencer (1965), for instance, found a positive relationship between homophily and selection of a personal source for consumer services (i.e., physicians). Brown and Reingen (1987) examined word of mouth referral behavior of piano teacher selection, and found that homophilous sources of information were more likely to be utilized, thus activating homophilous ties.

They also suggest that homophilous sources will be perceived a more credible than heterophilous ones and thus have greater influence on behavior (Brown and Reingen, 1987). McCroskey, Richmond, and Daly's (1975) development of a measure of perceived homophily in interpersonal communication provides a useful framework for understanding interpersonal similarity in human communication. They created a fourteen-item bipolar scale encompassing four dimensions of perceived homophily: Attitude, Background, Morality, and Appearance. In Gilly's *et al.,* (1998) dyadic study of interpersonal information search, homophily was operationalized in terms of two categories: demographic homophily (gender, education, and age) and perceptual homophily (values and experiences) of seeker and source. Gilly *et al.,* (1998) found a positive relationship between perceptual homophily and word of mouth influence. Demographic homophily, however, was found to be inversely related to the influence of word of mouth communication.

In the cyber world, information and discussions on a variety of topics are presented and available on the Internet. Despite the diversity of Internet users in general, consumers online are able to freely select their exposure to certain topics and participate in virtual communities, and thus control their social interactions with consumers who share common ideas and interests (Best and Krueger, 2006). This perspective assumes that people tend to interact with similar individuals in an online setting. This control of social interactions increases homophily among consumers (Best and Krueger, 2006). In addition, a recent study conducted by Wang *et al.,* (2008) investigated whether users exhibit different evaluative mechanisms in utilizing health information presented in Web sites versus online discussion groups. The results of their study suggest that credibility and homophily are the two fundamental mechanisms for the social influence of online health information (Wang *et al.,* 2008). Specifically, homophily plays a significant role in determining credibility perceptions and influencing the persuasive process in both Web sites and online discussion groups. That is, higher levels of perceived homophily of an online health information stimulus lead to a higher acceptance of that particular information.

In the social networking site context, similar demographic characteristics, such as young and educated, characterize users on these sites (Solman, 2007). To my knowledge,

Thelwall (2009) recently published the first exploratory study pertaining to homophily in MySpace, one of the most popular social networking sites in the U.S. Thelwall (2009) examined whether social interactions on social networking sites inhibit or improve the offline phenomena that friendships tend to be formed between homophilious individuals. Findings from his study showed that although gender homophily does not exist, homophily for "ethnicity, religion, age, country, marital status, attitude towards children, and sexual orientation are reasons for joining MySpace." Although focusing on a single social networking site (MySpace), Thelwall's (2009) study provides an interesting observation with regard to homophily in social networking sites.

Trust

Trust in social networking site users is another social relationship variable that is conceptualized as an important factor influencing consumers' willingness to engage in electronic word of mouth in social networking sites. Trust has long been recognized as an important construct in communication and social relationships and has been defined and conceptualized in many different ways in existing literature (Couch and Jones, 1997; Gabarro, 1978). In general, trust can be viewed as an enduring attitude or trait (Deutsch 1958; Rotter, 1967), a behavioral intention or behavior which involves vulnerability and uncertainty of the trustor (Chow and Chan, 2008; Coleman, 1990; Deutsch, 1958; Giffin, 1967; Schlenker, Helm, and Tedeschi, 1973), or a transitory situational variable (Driscoll, 1978; Kee and Knox, 1970). Moorman, Deshpande, and Zaltman (1993), for example, define trust as "a willingness to rely on an exchange partner in whom one has confidence". This confidence comes from the partner's expertise, reliability, and trustworthiness (Moorman, Deshpande, and Zaltman, 1993). In other words, trust focuses on confidence in the behavior of the partner or an ability to predict his or her behavior (Carroll *et al.,* 2007; Gundlach and Murphy, 1993).

From this perspective, trust or interpersonal trust is viewed as an enduring and generalized attitude, belief, or expectancy possessed by an individual or a group in interpersonal relations that the statement or promise of another individual or group can be relied upon (Blau, 1964; Carroll *et al.,* 2007; Giffin, 1967; Rotter, 1967; Schurr and Ozanne, 1985). Along the same line of thinking, compared to anonymously reading comments via other electronic word of mouth formats (e.g., product review sites and forums); connections through social networking sites are embedded in consumers' own networks and may therefore be perceived as more credible and trustworthy than anonymous sources or marketers. Therefore, perceived trust in social networking site users is predicted to influence consumers' willingness to engage in electronic word of mouth via these sites.

Trust is frequently described as a crucial part of social capital (Adler and Kwon, 2002; Bouma, Bulte, and van Soest, 2008; Chow and Chan, 2008; Fukuyama, 1995; Onyx and Bullen, 2000; Putnam, 1993). For example, Fukuyama (1995) views trust as an important social value that is essential to social capital. According to Fukuyama (1995), trust is defined as ''the expectation that arises within a community of regular, honest and cooperative behavior based on commonly shared norms on the part of other members of that society." This definition is reflected in Li's (2007) recent work, suggesting that "trust is the expectation and demonstration of committed goodwill for social capital" and thus is a key for the creation of prosperity in society.

Several studies have contributed to the understanding of the role of trust in information exchange and knowledge integration (Pigg and Crank, 2004). For example, Leonard and Onyx (2003) argue that the level of trust plays a vital role in determining an individual's decision to bridge other networks to exchange information or other resources existing in social capital. Similarly, Nahapiet and Ghoshal (1998) suggest that trust facilitates the use of information because it increases the perceived credibility of information and thus leads to higher usage of that information.

Results from Robert, Dennis, and Ahuja's (2008) study further confirmed this finding, suggesting a positive relationship between trust and knowledge integration in digitally enabled teams. Collectively, trust affects information exchange and sharing as it allows individuals to justify and evaluate their decision to provide or attain more useful information (Kramer, Brewer, and Hanna, 1996). With a higher degree of trust, the amount and types of information exchanged increases (Andrews and Delahaye, 2000; Dirks and Ferrin, 2002). In the human communication context, trust between a source and a receiver is significant to the dissemination of information and knowledge, which could contribute to effective interpersonal communication in both offline and online environments.

As new communication technologies continue to develop, the Internet has become an important channel for consumers to share product-related information and experience with a brand. The anonymous feature of the Internet allows consumers to freely interact with other consumers online without revealing their true identity (Best and Krueger 2006). Recently, researchers have studied the social implications of the Internet and examined the relationship between Internet usage and interpersonal trust.

Some suggest that the anonymity of the Internet may increase consumer information accessibility by removing social barriers such as age and race, whereas consumers cannot develop interpersonal trust towards others because of unknown sources of information (Blanchard and Horan, 1998; Shah, Kwak, and Holbert, 2001). In addition, findings from Best and Krueger's (2006) study suggest that online social interaction is positively related to bridging social capital and thus enhances generalized trust, a relatively thinner trust compared to localized trust gained from bonding social capital. Because the Internet enables the geographic reach without boundary limitations, these online social interactions typically promote the development of weak ties but inhibit strong ties and thus increase generalized trust among Internet users from different groups or communities (Best and Krueger, 2006; Williams, 2007).

Given the increased popularity for participating in virtual communities in recent years, a few researchers have suggested that trust is essential for continuous participation in virtual communities (Jarvenpaa, Knoll, and Leidner, 1998; Lin 2006; Ridings, Gefen, and Arinze 2002). Ridings, Gefen, and Arinze (2002), for example, examined antecedents and effects of trust in virtual communities and measured two dimensions of trust -ability and benevolence/integrity. The results of their study showed that trust plays an underlying role in influencing members' intention to give and search information via virtual communities (Ridings, Gefen, and Arinze, 2002). Additionally, Lin (2006) identified behavioral intention to participate in virtual communities and suggests that perceived trust is one of the components of attitudes towards participation in virtual communities.

Interpersonal Influence

The next dimension that plays a significant role in determining consumers' engagement in electronic word of mouth in social networking sites is consumer susceptibility to interpersonal influence (Bearden, Netemeyer and Teel, 1989). Previous studies on word of mouth suggest that certain individual difference factors may be associated with word of mouth referral behavior in the traditional marketplace. For instance, individuals who value the interdependent self and focus on the importance of the social context may be more subject to the influence of word of mouth (Briley, Morris, and Simonson, 2000). Similarly, word of mouth may become the most powerful source of information when consumers are susceptible to interpersonal influence (Bearden, Netemeyer, and Teel, 1989).

Bearden, Netemeyer, and Teel (1989) argue that consumer susceptibility to interpersonal influence plays an important role in influencing consumer purchase decisions. Originating from McGuire's (1968) early work pertaining to personality and susceptibility to social influence, Bearden, Netemeyer, and Teel (1989) defined consumer susceptibility to interpersonal influence as "the need to identify with or enhance one's image in the opinion of significant others through the acquisition and use of products and brands, the willingness to conform to the expectations of others regarding purchase decisions, and/or the tendency to learn about products and services by observing others or seeking information from others".

McGuire (1968) defined consumer susceptibility to interpersonal influence as a general personal trait that varies across individuals.

Based on this underlying concept, Bearden, Netemeyer, and Teel (1989) later developed a scale to measure consumer susceptibility to interpersonal influence. Researchers over the years have suggested that interpersonal influences play an important role in influencing consumer decision making (Bearden, Netemeyer, and Teel, 1989; D'Rozario and Choudhury, 2000; Park and Lessig, 1977). Therefore, interpersonal influence is conceptualized and linked to the influence of social relationships on consumer reliance on social networking sites as a source of product-focused information.

Past studies have identified the dimensions of susceptibility to interpersonal influence and its impacts on consumer purchases. Deutsch and Gerard (1955), for instance, proposed that interpersonal influence could be manifested in two different forms, normative and informational. Bearden, Netemeyer, and Teel (1989) further examined these two types of influences in a purchase decision context. In this regard, normative influence can be further classified into value expressive and utilitarian influences (Bearden and Etzel, 1982; Bearden, Netemeyer, and Teel, 1989; Park and Lessig, 1977). Value expressiveness is motivated by the need for psychological association with a person or group, which reflects the acceptance of positions expressed by others.

The utilitarian aspect of normative influence, on the other hand, is associated with the attention to act in accordance with the wishes of pledges to achieve rewards or avoid punishments. Informational influence is related to the tendency to make informed decisions by accepting information from others (Bearden, Netemeyer, and Teel, 1989). Informational influence may be manifested through either consumers directly requesting information from knowledgeable others or indirectly making observations of the behavior of others (Bearden, Netemeyer, and Teel, 1989; Park and Lessig, 1977).

Through the process of internalization, informational influence occurs when consumers perceive that information from others increases their own knowledge, and thus exert impacts on product evaluations and choices (Bearden and Etzel, 1982; Bearden, Netemeyer, and Teel, 1989). In essence, normative influences play a determining role in directing and controlling "evaluations, choices, and loyalties," whereas informational influences play an influencing role in helping consumers in "product, brand, and store search" (Mascarenhas and Higby, 1993).

Consumer susceptibility to interpersonal influence has been proposed as a general trait that differs across individuals and is viewed as a two-dimensional construct-*normative influences* and *informational influences* (Bearden, Netemeyer, and Teel, 1989). Normative influences refer to the tendency to conform to the expectations of others and can affect attitudes, norms, and values (Burnkrant and Cousineau, 1975). Informational influences refer to the tendency to accept information from knowledgeable others and can help to guide consumers in product, brand, and store search (Bearden, Netemeyer, and Teel, 1989;

Deutsch and Gerard, 1955). While all consumers show some susceptibility to interpersonal influence, they vary in the degree of their susceptibility to interpersonal influence. Hence, interpersonal influence is also discussed as a potential social factor that relates to one's relations with others and influences electronic word of mouth behavior.

Given the above review of social relationship variables, it is apparent that individuals' relations with others may exert great impact on information sharing and exchange among consumers. Therefore, it is argued that social relationships of social networking site users may contribute to the nature of electronic word of mouth communications occurring on these sites. Because social networking sites can facilitate the establishment and maintenance of social relationships and thereby influence information giving and seeking behaviors online, this study describes social factors as fundamental dimensions in examining electronic word of mouth behavior in the highly social and collective social networking sites.

In summary, social relationship variables, including *social capital, tie strength, homophily, trust,* and *interpersonal influence* are conceptualized as important drivers that affect consumers' reliance on social networking sites as a vehicle for electronic word of mouth. By examining the impact of social relationship variables on electronic word of mouth in social networking sites, the nature of interpersonal communication in computer-mediated environments can be thoroughly understood. Given the influence of social networks in the diffusion of products and services (Brown and Reingen, 1987), social relationship variables may serve as important antecedents of electronic word of mouth in online social networking sites.

2.4 Electronic Word of Mouth within Social Networking Sites

The mounting use of social networking sites provides consumers with another social venue to search for unbiased product information and at the same time allows consumers to give their own consumption-related advice by engaging in electronic word of mouth. In particular, social networking sites enable consumers to share their experiences with products and brands with members in their social networks, either close friends or remote acquaintances. Electronic word of mouth in social networking sites occurs when consumers provide or search for informal product-related advice through the unique applications of social networking sites.

Through extensively social interactions on social networking sites, electronic word of mouth communicated via these sites may be especially effective given that these sites have provided an easy way for consumers to build and maintain robust social relationships online. Moreover, consumer-generated product-focused comments on social networking sites are available to Internet users around the world, which potentially exerts influence on consumers on a global scale. Consequently, social networking sites have become one of the most widely used online media of the existing electronic word of mouth formats. Regardless of the potential powerful influence of electronic word of mouth in social networking sites on brand communications, consumer behavior research has not examined the product-related electronic word of mouth behavior among social networking site users nor the resulting implications for advertising strategies.

2.4.1 Consumer Electronic Word of Mouth Behavior in Social Networking Sites

In social networking sites, consumers may engage in electronic word of mouth behavior through a variety of ways, such as posting their thoughts and opinions about a product or service on their personal profiles, sending product or promotional information through an inbox message (similar to email) within the sites, and adding applications like "Send McDonalds[2]" so that consumers can easily and quickly send free virtual gifts to their contacts.

More importantly, consumers can become part of a virtual brand community on social networking sites like "Addicted to Starbucks[3]" by joining the groups they selected. Participation in a virtual community can create a social benefit to a consumer for self-identification and social interaction, which may motivate consumers' engagement in electronic word of mouth communication to affiliate with and belong to online

[2] The McDonald's Corporation is the world's largest chain of hamburger fast food restaurants, serving around 68 million customers daily in 119 countries across 35,000 outlets.

[3] Starbucks Corporation, doing business as Starbucks Coffee, is an American global coffee company and coffeehouse chain and is the largest coffeehouse company in the world, with 23,305 stores in 65 countries.

communities (Balasubramanian and Mahajan, 2001; Hennig-Thurau *et al.,* 2004). In the case of social networking sites, consumers may write opinions on branded profile pages. Through participation in these communities, social benefits such as information exchange or emotional support from this community membership can be obtained (Balasubramanian and Mahajan, 2001; Hennig-Thurau *et al.,* 2004).

One of the notable differences between word of mouth and electronic word of mouth is that there is no differentiation between opinion leaders and opinion seekers for electronic word of mouth. The interactive nature of the Internet enables consumers to easily engage in electronic word of mouth and perform multiple roles, including opinion leaders, seekers, and forwarders. In online social networking sites, consumers may not only give product-related information and pass it on to others, but also obtain and seek advice from others for their purchase.

In summary, electronic word of mouth behavior within social networking sites may be initiated because of a desire to establish and maintain social relationships within consumers' personal networks. By passing along useful product information or sharing negative experiences with a product or company, social networking site users could help their contacts in their purchase decision-making. Likewise, by searching out advice and opinions from others, electronic word of mouth generated from social networking sites could exert impacts on users' product choices.

2.4.2 Characteristics of Electronic Word of Mouth Behavior in Social Networking Sites

One important characteristic of electronic word of mouth communication within social networking sites is that the personal networks are readily available, which leads social networking sites to become an important source of product information for consumers, especially college students, who comprise the largest segment of the social networking site population (Ellison, Steinfield, and Lampe, 2007). As social networking sites provide consumers with opportunities to efficiently create and maintain their personal networks, information sharing among consumers is rapidly becoming much easier and faster. Consumers who share consumption-related information on social networking sites may expect to gain immediate feedback from a specific contact in their personal network.

Unlike communicating with anonymous fellow consumers through other electronic word of mouth formats such as product forums, social networking site contacts are members in consumers' personal networks and are perceived as more trustworthy than unknown strangers. In sum, as soon as the new communication technologies make it possible for consumers to use social networking sites to connect with one another online, social networking sites may become an effective vehicle for electronic word of mouth among consumers and serve as an important source of product-related information and opinions.

Given that many companies now employ electronic word of mouth-based "Social Network Marketing" as part of brand communication strategies (Godes and Mayzlin, 2004; Strategic Direction, 2008), the potential impact of electronic word of mouth communication on consumer marketplace decision-making cannot be ignored. More importantly, examining the influences of social relationship factors on consumers' electronic word of mouth behavior in social networking sites is imperative for a theoretical understanding of the underlying process of online communications in social environments.

2.4.3 Conceptualization of Electronic Word of Mouth in Social Networking Sites

In the literature of marketing and communication, two important dimensions that affect the adoption and diffusion of new products have been identified- *opinion leading* and *opinion seeking* (Flynn, Goldsmith, and Eastman, 1996; Shoham and Ruvio, 2008). As previously mentioned, opinion leading and opinion seeking have been conceptually understood as two important components of social influences and word of mouth behavior (Goldsmith and Clark, 2008; Sun *et al.,* 2006). Opinion leading, specifically, has been frequently viewed as an important personality trait that affects the process of word of mouth communication (Feick and Price, 1987; Gilly *et al.,* 1998; Rogers, 1995). Individuals with high levels of opinion leading, also termed opinion leaders, may exert great impact on others' attitudes and behaviors (Feick and Price, 1987).

Lyons and Henderson (2005) examined opinion leading in a computer-mediated environment and found that online opinion leaders display higher levels of "enduring involvement, innovativeness, exploratory behavior, and self-perceived knowledge" than non-leaders. In the case of social networking sites, a socially extensive environment provides opinion leaders with greater opportunities to give product-related thoughts and opinions to other consumers. Opinion leaders may also use social networking sites as a tool for self-expression through associations with desired products and services (e.g., recommending a product).

Altogether, the exceptional growth of social networking sites offers opinion leaders a unique channel to strengthen their personal characteristics and enhance their ability and motivation for giving advice and recommendations to their fellows, which encourages the development of electronic word of mouth in social networking sites.

On the other hand, opinion seeking is the other related concept that plays a significant role in determining consumers' engagement in electronic word of mouth in social networking sites. In the traditional marketplace, opinion seeking is an important component of word of mouth communication because it can also facilitate the flow of information in the product diffusion process (Flynn, Goldsmith, and Eastman, 1996; Goldsmith and Clark 2008; Shoham and Ruvio, 2008).

Consumers with high levels of opinion seeking behavior, known as opinion seekers, tend to search for information and advice from others when making a purchase decision (Flynn, Goldsmith, and Eastman, 1996). Compared to opinion leaders, opinion seekers possess relatively lower product involvement and product class knowledge in a given product category, and therefore, opinion seekers actively look for information and advice from opinion leaders when they perceive the information to be useful (Goldsmith and Clark, 2008).

In computer-mediated communication research, Goldsmith and Horowitz (2006) measured motivations for consumer online opinion seeking. They found that opinion seekers seek opinions and advice online because it is easy to attain pre-purchase information and could reduce their perceived risk and secure lower prices (Goldsmith and Horowitz, 2006). In social networking sites, opinion seekers may regard the electronic word of mouth recommendations of friends or classmates as credible and reliable, and thereby rely on social networking sites as a source for their purchases.

Another important yet overlooked dimension of Internet-based electronic word of mouth is online *pass-along behavior* (Norman and Russell, 2006; Sun *et al.*, 2006). While Sun *et al.*, (2006) viewed behavioral consequences such as online forwarding and chatting as an outcome of online word of mouth, pass-along behavior is conceptualized as one of the dimensions of electronic word of mouth in this study. Because electronic word of mouth is defined as the behavior of exchanging product-focused information among peer consumers on the Internet, pass-along behavior that can affect the flow of information should be considered as a component of such electronic word of mouth behavior.

Furthermore, pass-along behavior is more likely to occur in an online context, as the unique characteristics of the Internet can facilitate information dissemination (Norman and Russell, 2006). By the same token, pass-along behavior is the natural component of electronic word of mouth occurring in social networking sites. In addition to giving or seeking information from friends or other contacts, pass-along behavior is a useful tool for social networking site users to exchange information about a product or brand.

In summary, *opinion leading*, *opinion seeking*, and *pass-along behavior* are significant dimensions of electronic word of mouth in social networking sites. Opinion leading is related to consumers' information giving behavior, whereas opinion seeking is associated with information seeking. It is vital to note that many opinion leaders may also be opinion seekers because of their desire for knowledge in a specific product class (Feick and Price, 1987; Lazarsfeld, Berelson, and Gaudet, 1944). Likewise, opinion seekers may also be opinion leaders when they possess high knowledge in a different product category.

As consumers become more connectedly linked by advancing technology of social networking sites, marketers must learn more about information exchange patterns of their target consumers in order to communicate effectively. By examining potential social factors that could drive the flow of information exchange, the process of electronic word of mouth occurring via social networking sites can be understood. Based on the above discussion on social relationship variables and electronic word of mouth, a general conceptual framework examining the relationships among these dimensions is developed. This study seeks to study the impact of social relationship variables on electronic word of mouth behavior.

Figure 2.1: Conceptual Framework (Impact of Social Relationship Variables on Electronic Word of Mouth Behaviour)

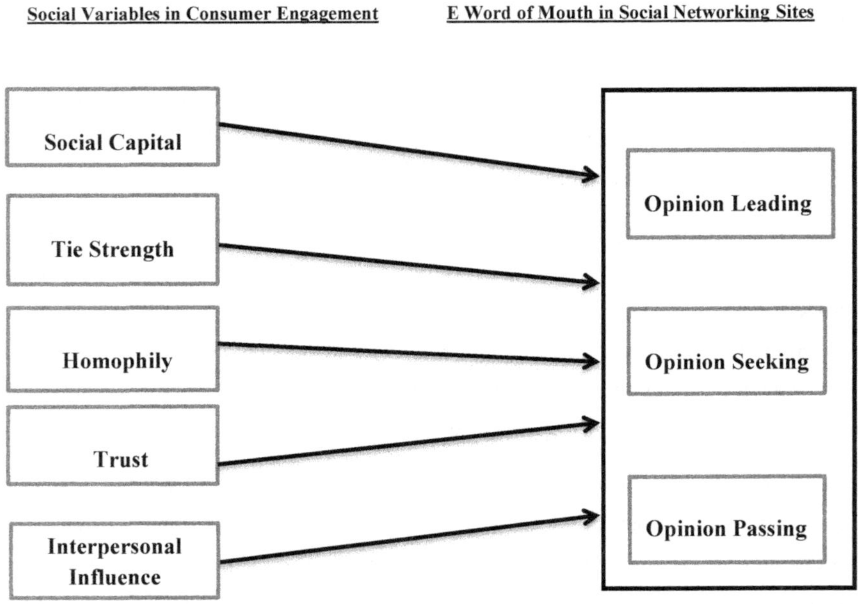

Adapted from Chu, Shu-Chuan and Yoojung Kim (2011), "Determinants of Consumer Engagement in Electronic Word-of-Mouth

Company Perspective

2.5 Integrating Social Networking Sites in Marketing Communication within Organizations

Marketing is often conceived as the process of identifying and meeting customer needs and wants over time. It tends to view technology as a means to the end of meeting user requirements. Certainly, this is how technology is both conceived and perceived in today's markets. The "marketing concept" tends to see technology in the form of products and services primarily as a means to the laudable end of producing a satisfied customer.

Internet has the credibility of immediacy and fastness, and brings globalization in every aspect of communication. Communication through internet is more specified, with effective interactive strategy among its users. India has about 120 million people online today—just 10 percent of its population. By 2015, however, there will be more than 330 million of them, making the country second only to China in the number of citizens using the Internet. *(Source: "India's Internet Opportunity" Report- Mckinsey, March 2013).* This expansion offers India an opportunity to transform its internet profile, to expand usage even beyond current projections, and to boost GDP substantially. One of the greatest uses of internet has been its usage in marketing communication. Promotion on digital platforms is gaining prominence.

In recent days, internet advertising has taken a new form which has more advantages over the traditional mediums like print media, television and radio. Marketing communication is becoming precise, personal, interesting, interactive and social. Different strategies of communication are followed in various social networking sites like Facebook, Twitter. They not only create impact over the audience, but also make them interact with the marketing statistics created. People get attached to brand communication in social networking sites than usual banner and pop up ads. These networking sites bring more interactive communication with advertising. Social networking sites will become the primary arena for highly targeted marketing and advertising.

Across various countries, social media penetration has reached a reasonable level for encouraging strong marketing initiatives. Given the global reach and interactive capabilities of social media, companies across key industries have started developing a social media marketing strategy with increased marketing budget allocations. The key influencers include direct access to a large user base of potential consumers, and insights into key changing trends and the thought processes behind buying decisions. Although it varies across industries, social media marketing's broad focus is on developing products targeted at specific consumer groups, launching new product offerings and monitoring brand image sentiments.

Now a days, technology is constantly changing, and when a brand is a part of the social networks, it is obvious that it is able to change with it. Social networks have become an increasingly important part of the online experience and are used daily by millions of people. Perhaps it could be so basic definition that social media is people having conversations online. However, with the basic definition, social media is an umbrella term that identifies the different activities that integrate technology, social interaction and the construction of videos, texts, audios and all types of pictures. These social media sites can be classified into three main areas: These are multimedia, communication and entertainment (Boyd and Ellison, 2007). In the subject of describing social media, McConnell and Huba (2007) suggest that it is 'the sum totals of people who create content online, as well as the people who interact with it or one another'.

Social media are tools that provide people with the ability to collaborate and communicate with one another online. Social media tools facilitate the creation and sharing of knowledge, information, media, ideas, opinions and insights, and allow people to actively participate in the media itself. This signals the move from passive consumption of marketing messages to facilitating interaction with messages.

Online tools include social networking sites, blogs, wikis, podcasts, content aggregators and content communities. Of these social media tools, social networking sites (social networking sites) and blogs have experienced the most prolific growth. Social networking sites account for nearly 17 per cent of total internet time. People are spending more time on social networking sites and do so at the expense of traditional media (McGiboney, 2009).

Hailed as a prospective new means of reaching and engaging consumers, Nielsen (2009) highlights that 'the social networks and advertising industry haven't yet found that magic formula to make this happen'.

Despite the increasing amount of time people are spending on social networking sites (McGiboney, 2009), these sites have yet to be harnessed as a successful marketing tool for reaching and engaging consumers (Nielsen, 2009). Social networking sites enable their users to create, build and maintain relationships that were not previously possible with a large and extended network of contacts. They can also provide a company with the potential to reach this large network of contacts (Enders *et al.,* 2008). As a medium that centres on communication between individual users, companies must employ a different approach if they are to engage consumers effectively via social networking sites (Gillin, 2007), as consumers are essentially using social networking sites to be social and to make themselves heard (McKinsey & Co., 2006).

The last few years have witnessed an explosion in media channels. Advertisers no longer face the traditional decision of "simply" choosing whether to expose their brands in broadcast media, print media, on the web, or on outdoor posters and billboards. Today, they may just decide to advertise on sheep, in golf holes, on bananas, or on face masks. These are just a few real-life examples of what Dahlén (2005) defines as "creative media choice", that is, employing a novel medium that makes a statement in itself. The creative media choice is based on an associative overlap with the brand so that the medium in itself (rather than the advertising placed in it) communicates the message.

According to Liu & Shrum (2002), emergence of new media (Internet) brought new models of interactivity: user-to-user message. Contemplating about user-to-user interactivity, Ha and James (1998) suggested that "the more communication in a computer-mediated environment resembles interpersonal communication, the more interactive the communication".

Steuer (1992) defined users-to-message interaction as follows: — "the extent to which users can participate in modifying the form, and content of a mediated environment in real time".

Commercial online services and the introduction of the web have created the potential for a mass interactive dialogue between exchange parties (Peters, 1998).

The world has witnessed the evolution of a universal interconnected network of audio, video, and electronic text communications; that blurred the distinction between interpersonal and mass communication and between public and private communication. The new market space changed the behaviour of the people and the communication models. The shift is then from a "one (firm)-to-many (consumers)" model of communication to the "many-to-many" model where contribution to the medium, and the message may come from both directions (Hoffman and Novak, 1996).

Chaffey (Dave Chaffey *et al.,* 2007) argues that such kind of communication allows mass customization and personalization, and the messages sent through Internet can be targeted more effectively.

The interactivity gains a new meaning when it is applied through web 2.0 platforms and social media channels as dialogue between consumer and company becomes much more active and interactive. As summarized in the media landscape analysis, the past decade was all about two-way communication's and interaction's models. Most of the marketing academics (Kotler, *et al.,* 2012) recognized the importance of creating two-way marketing channels between consumer and company for brand building, CRM, sales etc. Social media, itself, does not change this idea, but redefines interactivity and takes it to another level.

Armano (2008) argues that social media goes beyond the interactive marketing which is facilitated by computer-human interaction, and introduces human-to-human interaction enabled by technology. The main difference is that the companies instead of pushing the content (i.e. automated e-mails) through online channels empower people to engage and interact with other people and produce new content about the company (blogging, commenting, social networking , etc.). Free production of content and voluntary distribution is the key elements of the social media.

The User Generated Content (UGC) can become influential message of the consumer to the consumer (C2C) about the company and therefore should be carefully monitored. In fact, the content is the new message in social media channels. According to Eikelmann

(Eikelmann *et al.,* 2008), the best marketers can do in this environment is to try to engage with the consumers through social media in order to influence these messages. Drury (2008) suggests that instead of sending simple messages, marketers should provide the content which would be relevant for consumers and would generate conversations among them.

Marketers are forced to look for alternative communication strategies to market in the social media environment, because advertising clutter, growing advertising literacy and changing consumer behaviour drives down the return on investment (Biegel, 2008; Constantinides and Fountain, 2008). These strategies have to consider the increasing fragmentation in the markets. Unconventional marketing principals are effective because it considers the needs and wants of the people and listens to them. Therefore it aims to build a more in-depth and lasting customer relationship based on loyalty and trust.

Viral and word of mouth marketing principals are the essentials in social media. This medium provides a platform for web 2.0 applications and tools, which works as enablers in order to increase reach and speed of the messages. According to Lockhorn (2007), word of mouth campaigns can take off very quietly through niche communities and can be powerfully persuasive, or conversely result in an astonishing backlash.

The word of mouth (word of mouth) medium provides a "tool" which works as enabler in order to increase reach and speed of the messages. Word of mouth exchanges the information through the social media/networks in a global inexpensive publishing tool with those who want to participate in the Viral Capacity. Word of mouth seems very straight forward and simple to understand, yet elusive when we adapt social media technology on top of the consumer's ability to exchange and engage in issues of products. According to Lockhorn (2007), word of mouth campaigns can take off very quietly through niche communities and can be powerfully persuasive or conversely result in an astonishing backlash for a product, brand or services.

Word of mouth has a greater impact on product judgments, attitude formation and decision making that formal marketing communications (Herr, Kardes & Kim, 1991; Bone, 1995). The value of word of mouth marketing is a joint function of the receiver's involvement in the communication and the communicator's creditability (Hass, 1981). For marketers, understanding how word of mouth networks differ online is particularly pertinent in terms of web design and marketing communication strategy. What company marketers have to do is to embrace an empathetic approach during individual interactions and across all marketing touch points which can ignite word of mouth. All this can be summarized in two words, "Consumer Empowerment".

Consumer empowerment makes the consumers' voice louder in the viral network. Blogs have been created both for going into a positive interaction but also to confront and watch companies, ways of conducting their brands and products or for government laws. Word of mouth is fuelled by "positive" interactions across all the company's touch points, it happens both on a Macro (organizational elements, company policies, quality standards etc.) and Micro (experiences impacted by individual interactions) interactions. The type of Macro/Micro interactions stakeholders have with the company's product will have a big impact on whether word of mouth occurs and whether it will be positive or negative. On an almost daily basis, consumers exchange information/ knowledge which can expose cases of corporate misconduct or product defects which forces companies to respond. Web log postings of product and services problems often prompt a form of consumer activism called "blog swarms" (Gillin, 2007). These blog swarms frequently reach the mainstream media with significant consequence.

Blogging, podcasting, and other social media are profoundly disrupting the mainstream media and marketing industries. Paul Gillin's, "The New Influencers" explores these forces at work, identifying the new influencers, their goals and motivations, and offers strategies for both large and small organizations on how to influence the influencers.

Another interesting development in word of mouth is the increasing keenness of consumers to become part of the value creation process in terms of being a lead generator. Lead Generation appears when a company delivers on its brand promises, which leads to loyalty and trust from the consumers. When consumers start feeling the trust and loyalty towards a brand, they start to exchange their experiences and information by word of mouth to other people they trust and whom they happen to like. This exchange of information translates into referrals and sales leads.

The company will then benefit from word of mouth referrals because these include some inherent trust in the company's brand, which is passed on from influencers, which are not internal company marketers, but genuine costumers or consumers. Word of mouth marketing through social networks could emerge as an important tool in the marketer's arsenal. That will depend on whether marketers can tame the fundamentally unpredictable and serendipitous nature of word of mouth without losing what makes it so valuable in the first place – its authenticity (McKinsey, 2010).

This has led to a positive attitude towards the social media in all its forms and has created a visibility in the field and the term Enterprise 2.0 has also appeared in the literature (Bughin, 2008). Marketers and companies seem willing to engage in social media as part of their marketing strategy (Korica *et al.,* 2006; McKinsey, 2007; Forrester, 2007; Parise and Guinan, 2008). When an enterprise company wants to benefit from the new social media structure, they have to take into consideration how the interaction is done online from a costumer point of view. That is why new concepts as Consumer 2.0 and Enterprise 2.0 appear in the literature and in the marketing concept.

2.5.1 Social Media Networks as a Marketing Strategy for the Enterprise

A major change from conventional marketing perspective is the shift from persuasion to influence. Marketers should recognize that engaging social media networks is the best way to communicate with the increasing number of users/consumers who spend considerable part of their time on social media.

The online consumers are normally hard to reach with traditional push based or mass media based marketing methods (Forrester, 2007). The challenge of social media/ networks is the lack of experience and systematic research on the aptitude and effects of these applications. This means engaging social media/networks as part of a marketing strategy is still a trial-and-error process.

The theoretical fundamental for working professionals with social media/network is limited and hereby it is a pioneer job to find ways through which enterprises and marketers can extract value from social media network.

A number of authors have researched in different areas of where social media network has impact on the enterprise business. Swisher (2007) has searched the area of social media on the enterprise media asset management. Craig (2007) has searched the area of social media on learning environments and Anderson (2007) has described the commercial and organizational effects of social media applications.

Bernoff and Li (2008) have worked with the different ways enterprise departments can engage in social media networks without going into specific applications (Marketing, Sales, Customer Support, Operations).

To be able to gather the two approaches, it will be good to look at the issues from a dual perspective – from marketing and applications perspective combined.

Using the dual perspective, we can identify two main ways of engaging the social media networks as part of the company's marketing strategy: The Passive and the Active way. (Refer to Table 2.5)

Table 2.5: Dual Perspective of Engaging Social Media

Ways of engaging Social media	Description
The passive way or listening-in	Using social media networks as intelligence tool i.e. as source of customer voice and market information
The active way	Using applications of social media networks as PR, Direct Marketing and customer influence tool as well as a means for personalizing the customer experience and tapping costumer creativity.

Source: (E Constantinides, 2008)

The passive way of using social media networks can be recognized as a "top down" process where marketers collect intelligence from the consumers from listening to their voices of what they say online about the company, its products and competitors by monitoring the social media networks. This is not something new from a marketing perspective, never the less it is important to learn about the experiences the customers have with the company's products.

This way of collecting market information gives the company and its marketers the possibility to minimize the damage by having the opportunity to change/modify the products. Where do the marketers and companies find the voice of the costumers? Online blogs, forums and bulletin boards and even social networks are the places to monitor from a company's point of view. What is most important to know from a company's perspective is how valid and credible do the customers consider these applications.

According to Elliott (2002) and Bates *et al.,* (2006), costumers' experiences expressed in forums, blogs and product reviews is considered very credible by other consumers as this UGC becomes influencer on other consumers' attitude to the company and its products can be recognized as "vertical" communication (C2C). The entire viral exchange of experience and information can be an important determinant of success or the failure of a product, seriously disrupting costly marketing actions. Listening and collecting information from costumer's voice in a professional way can save time and cost in using traditional market research for this purpose.

The active way of using social media networks can be recognized as a "bottom up" (C2B) process where marketers actively engages in a dialog with consumers by launching a corporate blog or discussion forum. What happens in the bottom up process is that marketers do not own the message anymore. When the dialog is created with the consumers, the persuasion age is over and the new age of influence starts (Douma, 2008). This has been widely used by Steve Jobs, CEO of Apple and McDonalds Vice President, Bob Langert who daily used to post opinions on the corporate blogs, which encouraged the consumers to respond and exchange views and opinions. A variant of this strategy is when companies make employees publish content on the corporate blog. In fact content is the new message in social media network channels.

According to Eikelmann (Eikelmann *et al.,* 2008), the best a company and its marketers can do in this environment is to engage with the consumers through social media network in order to influence the message. This approach requires openness and trust of employee's capabilities (McAfee, 2006; Bryan *et al.,* 2007) and the company's products and communication – it has to be "pure and clean" when someone opens up for a dialog.

Next to company sponsored blogs, a simple low cost way to engage social media as PR is to use content communities – like a video sharing site, YouTube for distributing advertising material. One thing is for sure, companies and their marketers are forced to look for alternative communication strategies to market in the social media environment, as advertising literacy and changing consumer behavior diminishes the ROI (Biegel, 2008; Constantinides and Fountain, 2008).

2.5.2 The Changing Marketing Communications Environment

Companies are now witnessing a low return on investment due to increased advertising clutter, growing advertising literacy and changing consumer behavior. Marketers are forced to look for alternative communication strategies. Increasing fragmentation in the markets may shift the rules of targeting into behavioral marketing favor.

Indians are increasingly logging into their Facebook and Twitter accounts, with the country recording the highest social networking growth of 37.4% this year, according to a new study (Source: Emarketer: Social Network Users Statistics: India 2013 till 2017).

India will also have the world's largest Facebook population by 2016, research firm eMarketer found. Social media audience has become a hot area for organizations, brands and recruiters to reach their niche audience. With over one billion individuals, logged on to various social networks, people are now using social media for advice on what products to buy, where to shop and even what firms they want to work with.

There has been a strong social media adoption in India since past few years as the business organizations, government organizations and even political parties are actively utilizing the various social media platforms and social network sites to reach the people. A report released by the Internet and Mobile Association of India (IAMAI) and IMRB estimates 243 million internet users in the country by mid-2014, overtaking the US as the world's second largest internet base after China.

As per research undertaken by eMarketer, 75% of Indians who are internet subscribers, use social networking sites like Facebook, Twitter, YouTube, Pinterest etc. Interaction with friends, relatives, colleagues and community, live chat, status updates, image- as well as video-sharing are some of the major activities by Indians who spend close to 30 minutes every day online on the different social networks.

According to Internet and Mobile Association of India (IAMAI), 97 per cent of social network users are on Facebook. And they are spread beyond the big metros. One-third of social media users live in towns with a population of less than 5 million; 25 per cent of the total users live in towns with less than 2 million inhabitants. Social media usage is also fast catching up with mobile internet users. According to the report, 77 percent of the users access social networking on mobile phones. Email, social media, search, app store and chat / Instant Messaging are used every day by those accessing internet through mobile. Indians are very active on different social networks and are also actively increasing the amount of time they spend on the various social media.

Social networking sites can have powerful impact on organizations, if used systematically and innovatively. There are various benefits of integrating social networks into marketing communication within organizations.

Brand Recognition – One of the most powerful ways to use social media is as a brand-building tool. With social media, companies can decide how they want to position themselves and what they want people to know about what they do. With consistent efforts and great content, companies can build reputation for their brands around companies' values, benefits, and advantages.

Community – There is nothing like social media when it comes to cultivating brand communities. When the followers become part of communities, companies gain instant access to them. That means companies can find out what challenges followers are facing and what they like and don't like about product offerings. Companies can engage in on-going dialog that can be more valuable than any kind of paid market research.

Repeat Exposure – There is an old marketing adage that says it takes six to eight exposures to a product before a customer decides to buy. A clear benefit of social media is repeat exposure with a company's network. Companies have the opportunity to remind them over and over again about what is to be offered, which can shorten sales cycles dramatically.

Authority – For coaches, consultants, authors, speakers, and other service-based businesses, social media can be very powerful in helping establish authority in respective fields—making an individual the go-to resource for the target audience to seek out for help. Individuals can share great content, answer questions, and serve audience, and can inevitably build loyal fans.

Influence – As brand's following increases, company's influence grows. Having a substantial social media audience creates a snowball effect that can attract new customers, media interviews, joint venture partnerships, and all kinds of other opportunities.

Website Traffic – Many companies don't realize that social media can be a leading traffic generator. When brands share blog posts, videos and other content from websites, audience get reasons to click through and visit sites. Once there, companies have the opportunity to inspire those visitors to take action by inviting them to sign up for mailing lists, make purchases, or call to schedule free consultations. By installing traffic monitoring service, such as Google Analytics, social media can lead to building up traffic.

It has been shown that people with social media now have the opportunity to create and share their own brand related content. The user generated content has a direct impact on brand affinity and even sales, as consumers tend to trust other consumers over brand and hereby enterprises. Social media is changing the communication processes as the power shifts from enterprise to consumer and the meaning of the message itself is changing – content becomes the message.

A study found that consumers of social media don't want a controlled social media environment from the enterprise. Content relevance is a very important factor for the consumers and therefore becomes important for the enterprise. Consumers are afraid of losing time and privacy when participating in social media, but these communication push towards closer relationship with the enterprise and herby greater value for the enterprise.

2.5.3 Marketing through Social Networks

The evolution of social media marketing was determined in terms of an effective and efficient way of interactive communication. Keller (2009) states, "Interactive marketing communications allows consumers to learn from and teach others about a brand, as well as express their commitment to a brand and observe the brand loyalty of others". Social media plays a vital role and has already left an ever lasting impact in terms of brand equity.

Weber (2009) has approached the question of branding in the social web. He also defines this as the dialogue you have with your customer, and claims that the stronger the dialogue is, the stronger the brand is, and vice versa. Actually, he questions the very core concept of traditional marketing and branding, and means that rather than broadcasting messages to audiences and target groups, in the era of social web that we live in today, branding and marketing is about participating in social networks to which people want to belong, where dialogue with customers and between customers can flourish.

According to Weber (2009), marketing to the social web means to adopt a completely new way of communicating with an audience in a digital environment. Instead of continuing as broadcasters, marketers should become aggregators of customer communities. It is not about broadcasting marketing messages to an increasingly indifferent audience. Instead, when marketing to the social web marketers should participate in, organize and encourage social networks to which people want to belong. Rather than talking at customers, marketers should talk with them.

The task of aggregating customers is done in two ways: by providing compelling content on your web site and creating retail environments that customers want to visit, and by going out and participating in the public arena (Weber, 2009). Marketing to the social web is not only for the largest multinational corporations; it may be easier and more effective, argues Weber (2009), for a relatively small or medium-size company to take maximum advantages of the social media. Also the way of segmenting changes radically with the advent of the social web. Demographics like gender, age, education and income, lifestyle factors have become less relevant, and what really counts is segmenting according to what people do and feel- their behavior as well as their attitudes and interests. The goal for the marketer is to identify groups of customers within the larger market that can be reached and affected through the marketing (Weber, 2009).

As companies begin to realize the value of the Internet as a primary component of their communications platform, they are correspondingly beginning to leverage alternative marketing practices that are more cost-effective and more efficient at actively engaging with consumers, than traditional advertising channels. While the use of social media, guerilla tactics, and experiential campaigns are becoming more prevalent, best practices surrounding the strategic execution of these ever-evolving marketing tools and their incorporation into an integrated marketing communications (IMC) approach has not yet been robustly identified.

The effective use of alternative marketing practices can be especially advantageous for smaller to medium sized firms in the consumer products and services industry, which oftentimes lack the resources that are necessary for employing traditional forms of advertising. When integrated through a social media platform, viral, guerilla, and events-based marketing are cost-effective promotional options that can also deliver measurable business results. When developed in accordance with a company's overall strategic objectives, a smaller firm not only has the ability to communicate its message to its target audience, but also the ability to begin to cultivate meaningful relationships with its consumers.

Communication and information technology development has encouraged the emergence of new communication channels that have increased the options available to organizations for building relationships with clients (Albesa, 2007). Johnson and Greco (2003) explain that desires and different hopes from different clients can sometime require certain unique information and contact strategies. Communication channels and strategies now differ broadly from the ones in former times or offline times. It is important to understand the relationship between digital communications and traditional communication in the old media; for example, TV, radio, newspapers, magazines and billboard ads, the communication model was and is one-to-many compared to one-to-one or many-to-many communication model in digital media like blogs, social networks, wikis and other social media (Chaffey, 2003).

The increased fragmentation of media and customers, as well as the revolution in mass communication by the new communication channels – internet and mobile communication technologies – has created the need for a new approach to marketing communications that can ensure centralized management and a consistency of communication messages sent towards various audiences (McArthur and Griffin, 1997; Semenik, 2002; Smith, 2002).

The idea of integrated marketing communication (IMC) is to create consistency and synergy by combining marketing communication elements so that they support and enhance each other, to promote potential communication understandings (Duncan and Everett, 1993).

Social Media marketing is today seen by many practitioners as the new arena for market communication and on top of the list of users of the different mediums is Facebook, Blogs, Twitter, YouTube and LinkedIn (Steltzner, 2009). Kaplan and Haenlein (2010) define social media as —a group of Internet-based applications that build on the ideological and technological foundations of Web 2.0, which facilitates the creation and exchange of user generated content. It consists of different Internet applications such as blogs, social networking sites, content communities, collaborative projects, virtual game worlds and social worlds. Russell S. Winer (2009) affirms that many companies today are using some or all of the new media to develop targeted campaigns that reach specific segments and engage their customers to a much greater extent than traditional media.

Foux (2006) suggests social media is perceived by customers as a more trustworthy source of information regarding products and services than communications generated by organizations transmitted via the traditional elements of the promotion mix. Mangold & Faulds (2009) argue that marketing managers should comprise social media in the communication mix when developing and executing their Integrated Marketing Communication strategies and they presented the social media as a new hybrid element of promotion mix.

Mohan Nair (2011) takes social media as a complex marriage of sociology and technology that cannot be underestimated in its impact to an organization's marketing communications. The choice as to when to engage, how to manage and measure, and whether to lead or to follow is complex but not an impossible task. These cannot be answered simply by one formula because the context and the market dynamics are strong variables in these decisions. Even though the interest for social media is huge, few companies understand what the term —social media can mean to their businesses. But how much it has been given importance, as an IMC tool, varies from region to region (PricewaterhouseCoopers, 2009).

Even as organizations realize the need to engage customers at as many touch points as possible, there is still a need to stay ahead of the rapidly shifting marketing and communications landscape by integrating social media into traditional strategies to reach out to B2B and B2C audiences (Pownall, 2011).

Social media marketing is an engagement with various social media tools or any other online collaborative media to generate exposure, opportunity and sales. Social media marketing refers to the process of gaining traffic or attention through social media sites. Social networking sites allow individuals to interact with one another and build relationships. When products or companies join those sites, people can interact with the product or company. That interaction seems personal to users because of their previous experiences with social networking site interactions. Social networking sites such as Twitter, Facebook, YouTube, and blogs allow individual followers to "retweet" or "repost" comments made by the product being promoted.

Social media itself is a catch-all term for sites that may provide radically different social actions. For instance, Twitter is a social site designed to let people share short messages or "updates" with others. Facebook, in contrast is a full-blown social networking site that allows for sharing updates, photos, joining events and a variety of other activities.

By repeating the message, all the users who are connected are able to see the message, thereby reaching more number of people. Social networking sites act as word of mouth.

Because of the dissemination of information about the product through social networking sites, products/companies can have conversations and interactions with individual followers. This personal interaction can instill a feeling of loyalty into followers and potential customers. Also, by choosing whom to follow on these sites, products can reach a very narrow target audience. Social networking is a wonderful tool for establishing a brand.

A reputed brand always commands highest recall value among the consumers. And in today's context, nothing can help in building a brand better than social networking. Websites like Twitter, Facebook, LinkedIn, YouTube, and Friend Feed etc. have proved so crucial for building a strong brand name. These social networking sites are extremely useful in promoting company's products/services. People having a website, blog, or online business can do much better for themselves using above mentioned networking sites.

2.6 Research Gap

Consumer Perspective: Even though the findings of past research suggest the important role of social relationship factors in word of mouth in both the real and online worlds, it is unclear whether such antecedent factors affecting word of mouth communication may extend to electronic word of mouth in social networking sites. As social relationships are articulated and displayed in the form of contact lists or personal networks, consumers with highly connected social relationships are more likely to rely on information obtained from their contacts via social networking sites than consumers with their autonomous relations with others. Along this logic, differences in social relationships are predicted to lead to distinct electronic word of mouth behavior in social networking sites.

There is a dearth of research work in India, pertaining to the above topic. Thus a study is required to find significant predictors of electronic word of mouth behavior in social networks, in the Indian context.

Consistent with the ongoing argument, understanding the drivers of electronic word of mouth will not only contribute to the theoretical knowledge of interpersonal communication, but also help marketers in the development of promising brand communication strategies. Accordingly, this study focuses on social relationship dimensions that are frequently addressed in research on word of mouth to influence word of mouth behaviors. By linking social variables and electronic word of mouth, this study can help to develop a theoretically and empirically based framework of determinants of consumer engagement in electronic word of mouth in social networking sites.

Drawing from literature on social networks and traditional word of mouth research, a conceptual framework for social relationships and electronic word of mouth in social networking sites is developed. Specifically, social relationships among social networking site users are proposed as influential factors that drive consumers' engagement in electronic word of mouth in the importantly new social venue, social networking sites. As more consumers around the world rely on social networking sites as a source of product information, this investigation could contribute to literature on electronic word of mouth within the social media context and provide managerial implications for companies wanting to tap the power of social networks by incorporating electronic word of mouth programs in their marketing campaigns.

Company Perspective: Although the growth of social media marketing in the developing countries is promising, there are obvious challenges in reaching diverse customer groups from this marketing channel due to fragmented industries, low literacy rates and the relatively underdeveloped mobile infrastructure.

Despite the acknowledged impact of the internet on integrated marketing communication, very few studies have investigated the specific requirements and prospects for IMC in the online environment (Durkin and Lawlor, 2001; Reich, 1998). The increased fragmentation of media and customers, as well as the revolution introduced in mass communication by the new communication channels – internet and mobile communication technologies – has called for the need for a new approach to marketing communication (McArthur and Griffin, 1997; Semenik, 2002; Smith, 2002).

Pickton and Broderick (2001) claim that synergy is the principal benefit of bringing together the various aspects of marketing communications in a mutually supportive way.

From this perspective, marketing communication decisions should focus on the marketing communications channel that offers the highest benefit for all the stakeholders. Vollmer and Precourt (2008), addressed customers are turning away from the traditional sources of advertising, such as radio and television, and that they consistently insist on more control over their media consumption. Lindberg, Nyman & Landin (2010), examined how to implement and evaluate an online channel extension through Social Media, which compares and contrasts conventional marketing practices with social media marketing in the context of micro firms and then suggests these micro firms as which tools are more suitable for them.

This research will try to explore how digitalization and conventional media can co-exist within organizations. The study will further focus on identifying the current social media trends.

Chapter 3

Research Methodology

Research Methodology

Chapter Overview

Every research needs a methodology to direct its way towards a cogent and comprehensive goal. Thus a research methodology is the strategy, plan of action, process, or design lying behind the choice and use of particular methods and linking the choice and use of methods to the desired outcomes (Crotty, 1998).

This chapter details the statement of purpose, scope of the study, research objectives, research hypotheses and work plan for meeting research objectives. It also covers the essentials like method of structuring determinants, questionnaire development, sampling method and tools for analysis.

3.1 Statement of Purpose

The study primarily aims to assess the challenges and opportunities for social networking sites in India. The study will further establish an understanding of use of social networking sites by Indian consumers and organizations. The first part of the study aims to identify the profile of Indian consumers who use social networking sites. Further, it also examines the relationship between consumer engagement and electronic word of mouth (electronic word of mouth). A major study in this research focuses on five social relationship variables: social capital, tie strength, homophily, trust, and interpersonal influence that are related to electronic word of mouth behavior in social networking sites.

The study also aims to analyze the usage of social networking sites in marketing communication programs implemented by select marketing organizations. The research aims at finding out how social networking sites are used in different organizations with special reference to purposes of usage & metrics/measurement of effectiveness.

3.2 Scope of the Study

The present study has been conducted keeping in view the recent developments with respect to social networking sites around the globe. Social networking sites are playing a pivotal role in the marketing communication programs, and have been accepted as a marketing communication platform by consumers and companies.

This research aims to study the factors responsible for electronic word of mouth, which can further help the companies to formulate the marketing strategies based on electronic word of mouth behavior. The scope of this study is limited to the role of social variables and their effect on electronic word of mouth behavior.

This study is confined to the social relationship factors- social capital, tie strength, homophily, trust and interpersonal influence. The aim is to determine which social variables affect opinion seeking, opinion giving and opinion passing behavior on social networking platforms.

The scope of the study with reference to different sectors will identify the purposes of integrating social networks in marketing communication programs, and then identifying important metrics for measuring return on investment.

3.3 Research Objectives of the Study

Primarily this research aims to explore and study the challenges and opportunities for social networking sites in Indian context. For gaining clarity on the subject, the study has been divided into two parts.

Consumer Perspective: A study to gauge the attitude of Indian consumers towards social networks, and to study the impact of social variables on electronic word of mouth behavior.

The specific objectives of research for this part are as follows:

1. To identify the profile of Indian consumers who use social networking sites.
2. To explore the differences in consumer response to social variables vis-à-vis demographic variables of the respondents.
3. To study the impact of social variables (*social capital, tie strength, homophily, trust, and interpersonal influence)* on electronic word of mouth behavior (*opinion leading, opinion seeking, opinion passing)* in social networking sites.

Company Perspective: A study of use of social networking sites as a marketing communication tool, across select sectors.

The research attempts to understand the nature, and level, of social networking sites' usage by businesses and brands in India; its objectives and measurement. The research aims at finding out how social networking sites are used in different organizations with special reference to purposes of usage and metrics/measurement of effectiveness.

This part of the study has following objectives:

1. To study the importance and usage of social networking across select sectors.

2. To identify various metrics deployed to measure success of social networking sites across select sectors.

3.4 Methodology (Research Design, Research Instrument, Sampling, Methods of Data Collection)- Consumer Study

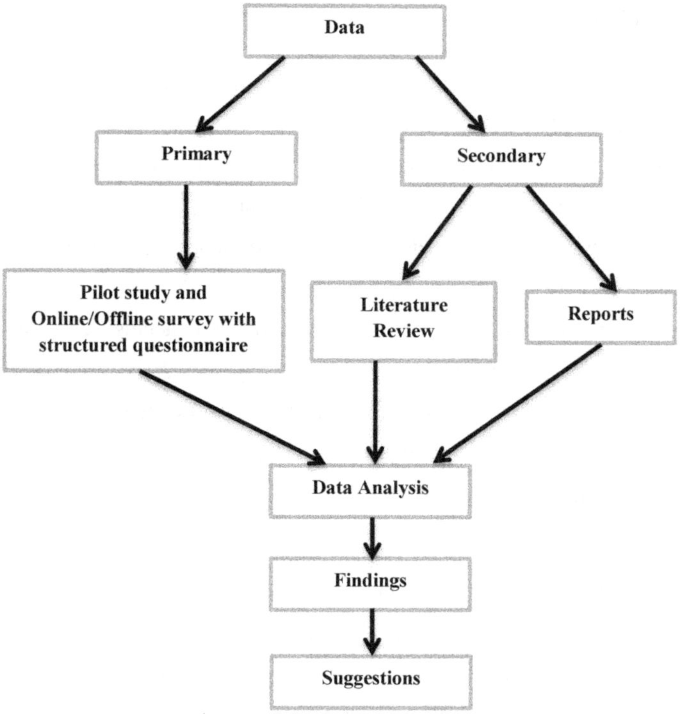

Fig 3.1 Research Design – Consumer Study ***(Source: Developed by Researcher)***

3.4.1 Research- Consumer Perspective

To Gauge the Attitude of Indian Consumers towards Social Networks, and to Determine Impact of Social Variables on Electronic Word of Mouth Behavior

To analyze the effectiveness of social networking sites among Indian consumers, it is important to study their attitude and electronic word of mouth behavior. A major part of the empirical study involved determining impact of social variables on electronic word of mouth behavior.

3.4.1.1 Research Instrument

The main objective of this consumer research was to identify the profile of Indian consumers who use social networking sites.

The other objective was to identify the determinants of consumer engagement in electronic word of mouth in social networking sites and to study the relationship between consumer engagement and electronic word of mouth (electronic word of mouth).

For achieving the first objective, demographic & psychographic details were found out through questionnaire. Segmentation of social networking sites users was done based on the usage rate, behaviour, attitude etc. Cluster analysis was used to segment different groups. For achieving other important objectives, a study of social variables affecting behaviour on social networks was carried out in second part of the questionnaire.

Pilot study was first carried out before running the actual survey. A pilot study is a small scale preliminary study conducted in order to evaluate feasibility, time, cost, adverse events, and effect size (statistical variability) in an attempt to predict an appropriate sample size and improve upon the study design prior to performance of a full-scale research project. Pilot studies, therefore, may not be appropriate for case studies. Pilot studies are frequently carried out before large-scale quantitative research, in an attempt to avoid time and money being wasted on an inadequately designed project. A pilot study is usually carried out on members of the relevant population, but not on those who will form part of the final sample. This is because it may influence the later behavior of research subjects if they have already been involved in the research.

A pilot experiment/study is often used to test the design of the full-scale experiment which then can be adjusted. It is a potentially valuable insight and should anything be missing in the pilot study it can be added to the full-scale (and more expensive) experiment to improve the chances of a clear outcome.

The self-administered online survey comprised questions assessing key constructs that investigate electronic word of mouth and social relationship variables on social networking sites. Items were adopted from prior research and were modified when necessary to fit the context of the present study.

The pilot study was conducted where the initial questionnaire was administered to 50 people, which included 28 faculty colleagues and 22 Post Graduate students. Corrections were done in the questionnaire after discussions. The questionnaire was further modified after final discussions with the research guide and other researchers. Based on the feedback and discussions, the measurement items were reduced to 47 from originally proposed 74 items. Appropriate changes were made in other questions as well.

Measurement Items

In the beginning of the questionnaire, use of social networking sites in general was explored to enhance the overall understanding of behaviors on social networking sites. Respondents were asked to indicate the social networking site that they visit most frequently from a social networking site list. Next, the questions also included measures of the duration, frequency, and amount of use of the site that the respondents undertook on an average day. Third, activities conducted and topics talked about on the site were asked. A five-point, Likert scale ranging from "not at all" to "to a very large extent" was used to examine the activities that respondents undertake on the site of their choice.

Respondents were asked to indicate the topics that they usually talk about on their favorite site from the following list: music, fashion, news, rumors and gossip, products or brands, political issues, college stuff, social events, and other. The respondents were asked to indicate that up to what extent, they get involved in interactions on SNS with the various categories of friends. This also gives an idea about the importance of weak and strong ties.

The second section of the questionnaire was designed to understand social relationships on social networking sites. The section included measures of five social relationship related variables- *social capital, tie strength, homophily, trust and interpersonal influence.* In the third section, social networking site users' engagement in electronic word of mouth was examined by assessing opinion leading, opinion seeking, and pass-along behaviors on social networking sites.

In the last section of the questionnaire, demographic characteristics such as gender, age, annual income, highest education and occupation were also examined. The specific measures are discussed as under:

1. Electronic Word-of-Mouth

Opinion leading, opinion seeking, and pass-along behavior were assessed to measure respondents' engagement in electronic word of mouth in their favorite social networking sites. Flynn, Goldsmith, and Eastman's (1996) opinion leading and opinion seeking scales were adopted. This measure consists of four items of an opinion leading scale and four items of an opinion seeking scale. Pass-along behavior was measured by adopting Sun *et al.,*'s (2006) four-item online forwarding scale. These items were modified to examine pass-along behavior on social networking sites.

Thus, a total of twelve items of opinion leading, opinion seeking, and pass-along behavior scales were used to examine electronic word of mouth in social networking sites. These measures were intended to gauge respondents' actual behavior with respect to electronic word of mouth. All of these items were measured by utilizing a five-point, Likert scale ranging from "strongly disagree" to "strongly agree." Respondents were asked questions regarding whether they provide, pass-along product-related information to others on the social networking site or they tend to seek advice from others.

2. Social Capital

Social capital was measured using scales developed by Choi *et al.,* (2008). Ten items were used to access social capital. As a result, five-point, Likert scale, with anchors of "strongly disagree" and "strongly agree" assessed social capital on social networking sites.

3. Tie Strength

The measures of tie strength were adopted from previous studies and included three questions about the respondents' social relation with contacts, the importance and closeness attached to the social relation (Brown and Reingen, 1987; Norman and Russell, 2006; Reingen and Kernan, 1986). Perceived importance and closeness were measured on five-point scales, with the endpoints of "not at all important" and "very important" and "not at all close" and "very close" respectively (Brown and Reingen, 1987; Norman and Russell, 2006).

4. Homophily

McCroskey, Richmond, and Daly's (1975) measure of perceived homophily in interpersonal communication was adapted to access perceived homophily of contacts on the social networking site. McCroskey, Richmond, and Daly's (1975) scale has been widely used in previous studies and has been found to be valid and reliable in different contexts (Wang *et al.,* 2008). Their scale is based on subjects' perceptions without the imposition of investigator interpretation and thus is considered to be objective. As a result, a seven-item, five-point Likert scale assessed this construct.

5. Trust

Trust was operationalized using five Likert items reflecting respondents' perceived trust in social networking site contacts. Responses on the trust scale were made on a five-point scale, with anchors of "strongly disagree" and "strongly agree." All of these items were adopted from previous studies and were modified for the purpose of the present study (Lin 2006; Mortenson 2009; Smith, Menon and Sivakumar, 2005).

6. Interpersonal Influence

The final construct of interpersonal influence was assessed by adopting ten items developed by Bearden, Netemeyer, and Teel (1989). Bearden, Netemeyer, and Teel's scale measures consumer susceptibility to interpersonal influence.

Appendix 1 provides the questionnaire used in this research.

3.4.1.2 Reliability and Validity of the Research Instrument

To validate the results empirically, appropriate reliability and validity tests of the measurement were taken. Indeed, reliability refers to the instrument's ability to prove consistent results in repeated uses, whereas validity refers to the degree to which the instrument measures the concept the researcher wants to measure.

This provides confidence that the empirical findings accurately reflect the proposed constructs (Flynn *et al.,* 1994). Measures of variables should have validity and reliability (Cronbach, 1971; Nunally, 1978) in order to draw valid inferences from the research.

Reliability: Reliability of a scale refers to how consistent or stable the ratings generated by the scale are likely to be. The most commonly used approach to measure internal consistency of a scale is Cronbach's alpha (Cronbach, 1951; Warner, 2008). Cronbach's alpha tends to be high if the scale items are highly correlated (Hair, *et al.*, 1998). According to Schuessler (1971), a scale is considered to have good reliability, if it has an alpha value greater than 0.60.

Reliability was assessed by calculating Cronbach's Alpha, a measure of internal consistency, for each measured scale. A reliable scale can produce consistent results when it is used by the same individual more than once or when it is used by a group of people who have the same attitude toward a certain concept (Rodeghier, 1996).
A scale can be considered acceptable if the value of the Cronbach's Alpha is 0.7 or greater (George & Mallery, 2003). The internal reliability of these measures was proven to be acceptable.

Table 3.1 Reliability Values (Cronbach's Alpha)

Independent Variables	**Cronbach's Alpha**
Social Capital	.836
Tie Strength	.848
Homophily	.842
Trust	.872
Interpersonal Influence	.900
Dependent Variables	**Cronbach's Alpha**
Opinion Leading	.901
Opinion Seeking	.888
Opinion Passing	.907

Validity: Validity of a measurement scale is the extent to which the scale fully captures all aspects of the construct to be measured (Parasuraman *et al.,* 2004; Hayes, 1998; Garson, 2002). In a general sense, a measurement scale is considered to be valid if it measures what it is intended to measure. Three types of instrument validity are generally considered for researches. They are content validity, convergent validity and discriminant validity.

Content validity also known as face validity, is defined as the extent to which the content of a measurement scale appears to tap all relevant facets of the construct it is attempting to measure (Parasuraman *et al.,*1991; Ding & Hershberger, 2002; Malhotra, 2008; Warner, 2008). It refers to the degree that the construct is represented by the items that cover the domain of meaning for the construct (Garver *et al.,* 1999; Malhotra, 2008).

Convergent validity is a form of construct validity which refers to the degree to which multiple attempts to measure the same concepts are in agreement (Garson, 2002; Warner, 2008). It deals with the question "do the items intended to measure a single latent construct statistically converge together" (Garver *et al.,* 1999). Operationally, convergent validity is assessed by the extent to which the latent construct correlates to items designed to measure the same latent construct.

Discriminant validity is assessed by the extent to which the items representing a latent construct discriminate that construct from other items representing other latent constructs (Garver *et al.,* 1999; Warner, 2008). It is also a form of construct validity but it represents the extent to which measures of different concepts are distinct (Malhotra, 2012). Convergent validity and discriminant validity form the construct validity.

In this research, the content validity of the measurement instrument was assessed by requesting subject experts to provide feedback. The expert panel of 15 included instructors and researchers from the disciplines of Advertising, Consumer Behavior, Branding, Digital Marketing and Behavioral Sciences. After they reviewed the questionnaire, based on their feedback, changes were incorporated to clarify and eliminate ambiguous statements.

The study employs widely used method of measuring content validity developed by C.H. Lawshe (1975). It is essentially a method for gauging agreement among raters or judges regarding how essential a particular item is. Lawshe (1975) proposed that each of the Subject Matter Expert raters (SMEs) on the judging panel respond to the question for each item: "Is the skill or knowledge measured by this item 'essential', 'useful but not essential', or 'not necessary' to the performance of the construct?" According to Lawshe (1975), if more than half the panelists indicate that an item is essential, that item has at least some content validity.

Greater levels of content validity exist as larger numbers of panelists agree that a particular item is essential. Using these assumptions, Lawshe developed a formula termed the content validity ratio: $CVR = (n_e - N/2)/ N/2$, where CVR= content validity ratio, n_e = number of SME panelists indicating 'essential', N= total number of SME panelists. This formula yields values which range from +1 to -1; positive values indicate that at least half the SMEs rated the item as essential. The mean CVR across items may be used as an indicator of overall test content validity. The minimum values of the CVR to ensure that agreement is unlikely to be due to chance can be found in the table 3.2:

Table 3.2: Minimum Content Validity Ratio (CVR Requirements)

Number of Panelists	5	6	7	8	9	10	11	12	13	14	15	20	25	30
Minimum Value	1.0	1.0	1.0	0.9	0.8	0.6	0.6	0.6	0.5	0.5	0.5	0.4	0.4	0.3

(Adapted from: Lawshe, 1975)

Any item, which is perceived to be essential by more than half of the panelists, has some degree of content validity and as more panelists (beyond 50%) perceive the item as essential, the degree of content validity increases. CVR for most items in the present study ranged from 0.60 to 0.74. Items with CVR below 0.5 were dropped from the questionnaire.

3.4.1.3 Sampling and Data Collection

It would normally be impractical to study a whole population, for example when doing a questionnaire survey. Sampling is a method that allows researchers to infer information about a population, without having to investigate every individual. Reducing the number of individuals in a study reduces the cost and workload, and may make it easier to obtain high quality information, but this has to be balanced against having a large enough sample size with enough power to detect a true association.

The most common sampling techniques used are:

Simple random sampling

In this case each individual is chosen entirely by chance and each member of the population has an equal chance, or probability, of being selected. One way of obtaining a random sample is to give each individual in a population a number, and then use a table of random numbers to decide which individuals to include.

Systematic sampling

Individuals are selected at regular intervals from a list of the whole population. The intervals are chosen to ensure an adequate sample size. For example, every 10th member of the population is included. This is often convenient and easy to use, although it may also lead to bias for reasons outlined below.

Stratified sampling

In this method, the population is first divided into sub-groups (or strata) who all share a similar characteristic. It is used when we might reasonably expect the measurement of interest to vary between the different sub-groups. Gender or smoking habits would be examples of strata. The study sample is then obtained by taking samples from each stratum.

In a stratified sample, the probability of an individual being included varies according to known characteristics, such as gender, and the aim is to ensure that all sub-groups of the population that might be of relevance to the study are adequately represented. The fact that the sample was stratified should be taken into account at the analysis stage.

Clustered sampling

In a clustered sample, sub-groups of the population are used as the sampling unit, rather than individuals. The population is divided into sub-groups, known as clusters, and a selection of these are randomly selected to be included in the study. All members of the cluster are then included in the study. Clustering should be taken into account in the analysis.

Quota sampling

This method of sampling is often used by market researchers. Interviewers are given a quota of subjects of a specified type to attempt to recruit. For example, an interviewer might be told to go out and select 20 adult men and 20 adult women, 10 teenage girls and 10 teenage boys so that they could interview them about their television viewing. There are several flaws with this method, but most importantly it is not truly random.

Convenience sampling

Convenience sampling is perhaps the easiest method of sampling, because participants are selected in the most convenient way, and are often allowed to choose or volunteer to take part. Good results can be obtained, but the data set may be seriously biased, because those who volunteer to take part may be different from those who choose not to.

Snowball sampling

This method is commonly used in social sciences when investigating hard to reach groups. Existing subjects are asked to nominate further subjects known to them, so the sample increases in size like a rolling snowball. For example, when carrying out a survey of risk behaviors amongst intravenous drug users, participants may be asked to nominate other users to be interviewed.

This study basically used convenience sampling technique primarily because the nature of the study was exploratory and this technique was easy to use.

Convenience sampling is a non-probability sampling technique where subjects are selected because of their convenient accessibility and proximity to the researcher. In all forms of research, it would be ideal to test the entire population, but in most cases, the population is just too large that it is impossible to include every individual. This is the reason why most researchers rely on sampling techniques like convenience sampling, the most common of all sampling techniques. Many researchers prefer this sampling technique because it is fast, inexpensive, easy and the subjects are readily available.

Researchers use convenience sampling not just because it is easy to use, but because it also has other research advantages. In pilot studies, convenience sample is usually used because it allows the researcher to obtain basic data and trends regarding his study without the complications of using a randomized sample.

This sampling technique is also useful in documenting that a particular quality of a substance or phenomenon occurs within a given sample. Such studies are also very useful for detecting relationships among different phenomena.

Sampling Procedure- Consumer Study

As a rule of thumb, data from at least 300 cases is considered comfortable, 500 is considered as very good and 1000 is considered excellent (Comrey & Lee, 1992 and Tabachnich *et al.,* 2012). Thus it was decided to target at least 500 respondents. Keeping in mind the nature of the study, a response rate of 55-60% was anticipated and thus, it was decided to administer questionnaires to around 1000-1100 respondents.

An online survey approach was used to address the research objectives of this study. While Indians primarily use the internet for communication, largely in the form of email, social media is also an important driver of internet use in India. Facebook users formed the respondents for this study, as this social media platform is most engaging, and so has attracted maximum internet users in India, till date.

It has been studied that young people are active users of social networks. Social networking site users are characterized as young, better-educated, and are disproportionately composed of college students (Ellison, Steinfield, and Lampe 2007; Fallows 2007; Lenhart 2009).

Keeping this in mind, the sampling technique used in this study was purposive convenience sampling. Finally, an online questionnaire was sent across around 1050 users of Facebook and a few on LinkedIn, of which 590 responded to the survey. Excluding the incomplete questionnaires, a total of 566 respondents were included in the study. The respondents were taken from my friends' list on Facebook, which formed the sampling frame for this study.

Facebook was prominently used for reaching respondents, as this platform was most appropriate to understand attitude towards social networks, and also to gauge electronic word of mouth behavior. Moreover, as there are more than 100 million Facebook users in India, the use of Facebook as the sampling frame was justified.

The questionnaire was self- prepared with help of chain references from a study conducted by Shu-Chuan Chu, 2009, titled "Determinants of Consumer Engagement in Electronic Word-of-Mouth in Social Networking Sites".

The entire data collection period was about nine months from June 2012 to February 2013.

3.4.1.5 Factor Analysis

Exploratory Factor Analysis

This test was being carried out for the survey related to the consumer study. Initially, exploratory factor analysis was conducted followed by confirmatory factor analysis conducted using AMOS 20 software. Table 3.3 shows the result of KMO and Bartlett's test, which is run to know the significance of factor analysis. KMO value was found to be .912, which is greater than 0.6 and significance was .000, which is less than 0.05. These values indicate that factor analysis is significant.

Table 3.3: KMO and Bartlett's Test

Kaiser-Meyer-Olkin Measure of Sampling Adequacy		.912
Bartlett's Test of Sphericity	Approx. Chi-Square	16485.443
	Df	1081
	Sig.	.000

Table 3.4: Total Variance Explained

Component	Initial Eigenvalues			Extraction Sums of Squared Loadings			Rotation Sums of Squared Loadings		
	Total	**% of Variance**	**Cumulative %**	**Total**	**% of Variance**	**Cumulative %**	**Total**	**% of Variance**	**Cumulative %**
1	12.839	27.318	27.318	12.839	27.318	27.318	4.953	10.539	10.539
2	4.457	9.483	36.801	4.457	9.483	36.801	4.281	9.110	19.649
3	3.120	6.638	43.439	3.120	6.638	43.439	3.907	8.313	27.962
4	2.489	5.296	48.735	2.489	5.296	48.735	3.643	7.751	35.712
5	2.111	4.491	53.226	2.111	4.491	53.226	3.345	7.118	42.830
6	1.770	3.766	56.992	1.770	3.766	56.992	2.686	5.715	48.546
7	1.362	2.897	59.889	1.362	2.897	59.889	2.607	5.547	54.093
8	1.299	2.763	62.652	1.299	2.763	62.652	2.467	5.250	59.342
9	1.257	2.674	65.327	1.257	2.674	65.327	2.016	4.290	63.633
10	1.113	2.368	67.695	1.113	2.368	67.695	1.909	4.062	67.695

Extraction Method: Principal Component Analysis.

Variance table 3.4 shows the percentage of variance explained by the extracted factors. The analysis extracted ten factors having percentage cumulative variance of 67.695%. This indicates that ten factors framework explained nearly 68% variations in this study. These ten extracted factors are: social capital, tie strength, attitude homophily, background homophily, trust, normative influence, informational influence, opinion leading behavior, opinion seeking behavior, opinion passing behavior.

The results of the factor loading were calculated and all statements were found to have factor loadings more than 0.4. The high factor loading, as mentioned in table 3.5 gives us an idea that no statement is further dropped on this basis, hence could be considered.

Table 3.5: Factor Loadings of Measurement Items

S. No.	Measurement Item	Factor Loading
1	Interacting with people on the social networking sites makes me interested in things that happen outside of my town.	.699
2	Interacting with people on the social networking sites makes me want to try new things.	.666
3	Interacting with people on the social networking sites makes me interested in what people different from me are thinking.	.763
4	Talking with people on the social networking sites makes me curious about other places in the world.	.723
5	Interacting with people on the social networking sites makes me feel like part of a larger community.	.537
6	Interacting with people on the social networking sites makes me feel connected to the bigger picture.	.509
7	Interacting with people on the social networking sites reminds me that everyone in the world is connected.	.438
8	I am willing to spend time to support general community activities on the social networking sites.	.402
9	Interacting with people on the social networking sites gives me new people to talk to.	.797
10	I come in contact with new people on the social networking sites all the time.	.828
11	Think like me	.820
12	Behave like me	.807
13	Are similar to me	.781
14	Are from social class similar to mine	.802
15	Are from economic class like mine	.889
16	Have status like mine	.815
17	Have moral values like mine	.423
18	I feel confident about having discussions with my friends on the social networking sites.	.714
19	The friends on the social networking sites will do everything within their capacity to help others.	.614
20	I trust most of my friends on the social networking sites.	.823
21	I have confidence in my friends on the social networking sites.	.877
22	My friends on the social networking sites offer honest opinions.	.798
23	I can believe in my friends on the social networking sites.	.851
24	I often persuade my friends on the social networking sites to buy products that I like.	.793
25	My friends on the social networking sites pick their products based on what I have told them.	.765

26	On the social networking sites, I often influence my friends' opinions about products.	**.756**
27	When they choose products, my friends on the social networking sites turn to me for advice.	**.709**
28	I ask my friends on the social networking sites about what products to buy.	**.566**
29	I like to get my friends' opinions on the social networking sites before I buy new products.	**.566**
30	I feel more comfortable choosing products when I have gotten my friends' opinions on them on the social networking sites.	**.508**
31	I take purchase decisions based on my friends' opinion & experiences.	**.424**
32	I tend to pass on information or opinion about the products to my friends on the social networking sites when I find it useful.	**.767**
33	When I receive product related information or opinion from a friend, I will pass it along to others on the social networking sites.	**.801**
34	I tend to pass along my friends' positive reviews on products to others on the social networking sites.	**.813**
35	I tend to pass along my friends' negative reviews on products to others on the social networking sites.	**.763**
36	I rarely purchase the latest fashion styles until I am sure my friends approve of them.	**.570**
37	It is important that others like the products and brands I buy.	**.778**
38	When buying products, I generally purchase those brands that I think others will approve of.	**.855**
39	If other people can see me using a product, I often purchase the brand they expect me to buy.	**.821**
40	I like to know what brands and products make good impressions on others.	**.734**
41	I achieve a sense of belonging by purchasing the same products and brands that others purchase.	**.781**
42	If I want to be like someone, I often try to buy the same brands that they buy.	**.687**
43	If I have little experience with a product, I often ask my friends about the product.	**.823**
44	I often consult other people to help choose the best alternative available from a product class.	**.808**
45	I frequently gather information from friends or family about a product before I buy.	**.798**
46	Overall, how important do you feel about your friends on SNS?	**.791**
47	Overall, how close do you feel to your friends on SNS?	**.767**

Confirmatory Factor Analysis

Confirmatory Factor Analysis (CFA) was used to examine the reliability and validity, whether the measures of a construct were consistent with the researcher's understanding of the nature of that construct (or factor). The measurement model included 47 items.

Exploratory Factor Analysis revealed 7 independent social variables. After that Confirmatory Factor Analysis (CFA) was conducted using AMOS 20. CFA is used to confirm the exploratory factor model by determining the goodness of fit between hypothesized model and sample data.

One of the primary objectives of this study was to examine the potential determinants of electronic word of mouth communicated via social networking sites. It was proposed initially that five social relationship factors: social capital, tie strength, homophily, trust, and consumer susceptibility to interpersonal influence will lead to consumers' engagement in electronic word of mouth communications in social networking sites. After EFA results, seven social variables were categorized and the research model was reframed.

Homophily was divided into two categories, attitude and background homophily, as explained in the literature review. Interpersonal influence was categorized into normative and informational influence.

Figure 3.2: Reframed Conceptual Framework

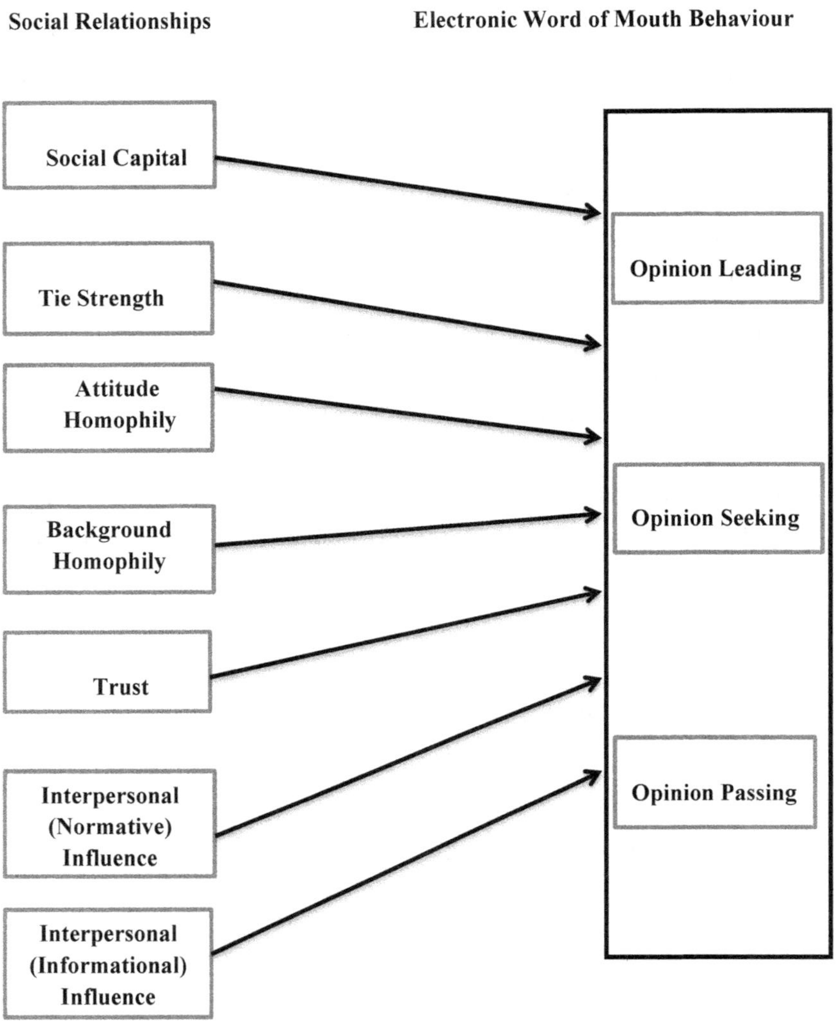

Model Fit Summary- Values Considered in Confirmatory Factor Analysis

CMIN: The Chi-Square value is the traditional measure for evaluating overall model fit and, 'assesses the magnitude of discrepancy between the sample and fitted covariance's matrices' (Hu and Bentler, 1999). A good model fit would provide an insignificant result at a 0.05 threshold (Barrett, 2007), thus the Chi-Square statistic is often referred to as either a 'badness of fit' (Kline, 2005) or a 'lack of fit' (Mulaik *et al.,* 1989) measure. While the Chi-Squared test retains its popularity as a fit statistic, there exist a number of severe limitations in its use.

Firstly, this test assumes multivariate normality and severe deviations from normality may result in model rejections even when the model is properly specified (McIntosh, 2006). Secondly, because the Chi-Square statistic is in essence a statistical significance test it is sensitive to sample size which means that the Chi-Square statistic nearly always rejects the model when large samples are used (Bentler and Bonnet, 1980; Jöreskog and Sörbom, 1993).

On the other hand, where small samples are used, the Chi-Square statistic lacks power and because of this may not discriminate between good fitting models and poor fitting models (Kenny and McCoach, 2003). Due to the restrictiveness of the Model Chi-Square, researchers have sought alternative indices to assess model fit. One example of a statistic that minimises the impact of sample size on the Model Chi-Square is Wheaton *et al.,'s* (1977) relative/normed chi-square ($\chi2$/df). Although there is no consensus regarding an acceptable ratio for this statistic, recommendations range from as high as 5.0 (Wheaton *et al.,* 1977) to as low as 2.0 (Tabachnick and Fidell, 2007).

Table 3.6: CMIN Value

Model	NPAR	CMIN	DF	P	CMIN/DF
Default model	168	2167.584	777	.000	2.790
Saturated model	945	.000	0		
Independence model	84	15755.131	861	.000	18.299

From the first set of fit statistics, CMIN (minimum discrepancy), it is observed that the chi-square value is 2167.584 at 777 degrees of freedom. The corresponding p value is .000. The CMIN/DF (normed chi-square) shows a value of 2.790, which is well within the acceptable level of 1.0 to 5.0. (Less than 1.0 is a poor model fit: more than 5.0 reflects a need for improvement)

Root Mean Square Residual (RMR) and Standardized Root Mean Square Residual (SRMR): The RMR and the SRMR are the square root of the difference between the residuals of the sample covariance matrix and the hypothesized covariance model. The range of the RMR is calculated based upon the scales of each indicator, therefore, if a questionnaire contains items with varying levels (some items may range from 1 – 5 while others range from 1 – 7), the RMR becomes difficult to interpret (Kline, 2005).

The standardized RMR (SRMR) resolves this problem and is therefore much more meaningful to interpret. Values for the SRMR range from zero to 1.0 with well-fitting models obtaining values less than .05 (Byrne, 1998; Diamantopoulos and Siguaw, 2000), however values as high as 0.08 are deemed acceptable (Hu and Bentler, 1999). An SRMR of 0 indicates perfect fit but it must be noted that SRMR will be lower when there is a high number of parameters in the model and in models based on large sample sizes.

Goodness-of-Fit Statistic (GFI) and the Adjusted Goodness-of-Fit Statistic (AGFI): The Goodness-of-Fit statistic (GFI) was created by Jöreskog and Sorbom as an alternative to the Chi-Square test and calculates the proportion of variance that is accounted for by the estimated population covariance (Tabachnick and Fidell, 2007). By looking at the variances and covariances accounted for by the model it shows how closely the model comes to replicating the observed covariance matrix (Diamantopoulos and Siguaw, 2000). This statistic ranges from 0 to 1 with larger samples increasing its value.

When there are a large number of degrees of freedom in comparison to sample size, the GFI has a downward bias (Sharma *et al.*, 2005). In addition, it has also been found that the GFI increases as the number of parameters increases (MacCallum and Hong, 1997) and also has an upward bias with large samples (Bollen, 1990; Miles and Shevlin, 1998). Traditionally an omnibus cut-off point of 0.90 has been recommended for the GFI however, simulation studies have shown that when factor loadings and sample sizes are low a higher cut-off of 0.95 is more appropriate (Miles and Shevlin, 1998).

Given the sensitivity of this index, it has become less popular in recent years and it has even been recommended that this index should not be used (Sharma *et al.,* 2005). Related to the GFI is the AGFI which adjusts the GFI based upon degrees of freedom, with more saturated models reducing fit (Tabachnick and Fidell, 2007). Thus, more parsimonious models are preferred while penalized for complicated models. In addition to this, AGFI tends to increase with sample size. As with the GFI, values for the AGFI also range between 0 and 1 and it is generally accepted that values of 0.90 or greater indicate well-fitting models. Given the often detrimental effect of sample size on these two fit indices they are not relied upon as a stand-alone index, however given their historical importance they are often reported in covariance structure analyses.

Table 3.7: RMR, GFI, AGFI, PGFI

Model	RMR	GFI	AGFI	PGFI
Default model	.060	.837	.811	.720
Saturated model	.000	1.000		
Independence model	.272	.213	.175	.203

RMR (Root mean square residual) are best interpreted in the metric of the correlation matrix. The standardized RMR, then, represents the average value across all standardized residuals. In a well-fitting model, this value shall be less than 0.08. The RMR value is .060 which is within the acceptable for the goodness of model fit.

For both GFI (Goodness of fit index) and AGFI (Adjusted goodness of fit index) indices values close to 1.00 are indicative of good fit. Based on the GFI and AGFI values of .837 & .811 respectively, it can be concluded that the hypothesized model fits the sample data quiet well.

Typically, parsimony based indices having lower values than the threshold level are generally perceived as acceptable for other normed indices of fit. In this study a PGFI (Parsimony goodness of fit index) value of .720 accompanied by goodness-of-fit indices in the .90s can be considered to be consistent.

Baseline Comparisons

Incremental fit indices: Incremental fit indices, also known as comparative (Miles and Shevlin, 2007) or relative fit indices (McDonald and Ho, 2002), are a group of indices that do not use the chi-square in its raw form but compare the chi-square value to a baseline model. For these models the null hypothesis is that all variables are uncorrelated (McDonald and Ho, 2002).

Normed-fit index (NFI): The first of these indices to appear in LISREL output is the Normed Fit Index (NFI: Bentler and Bonnet, 1980). This statistic assesses the model by comparing the $\chi 2$ value of the model to the $\chi 2$ of the null model. The null/independence model is the worst case scenario as it specifies that all measured variables are uncorrelated. Values for this statistic range between 0 and 1 with Bentler and Bonnet (1980) recommending values greater than 0.90 indicating a good fit. More recent suggestions state that the cut-off criteria should be NFI $\geq$ .95 (Hu and Bentler, 1999).

A major drawback to this index is that it is sensitive to sample size, underestimating fit for samples less than 200 (Mulaik *et al.,* 1989; Bentler, 1990), and is thus not recommended to be solely relied on (Kline, 2005). This problem was rectified by the Non-Normed Fit Index (NNFI, also known as the Tucker-Lewis index), an index that prefers simpler models. However in situations where small samples are used, the value of the NNFI can indicate poor fit despite other statistics pointing towards good fit (Bentler, 1990; Kline, 2005; Tabachnick and Fidell, 2007). A final problem with the NNFI is that due to its non-normed nature, values can go above 1.0 and can thus be difficult to interpret (Byrne, 1998). Recommendations as low as 0.80 as a cutoff have been proffered however Bentler and Hu (1999) have suggested NNFI $\geq$ 0.95 as the threshold.

CFI (Comparative fit index): The Comparative Fit Index (CFI: Bentler, 1990) is a revised form of the NFI which takes into account sample size (Byrne, 1998) that performs well even when sample size is small (Tabachnick and Fidell, 2007). This index was first introduced by Bentler (1990) and subsequently included as part of the fit indices in his EQS program (Kline, 2005). Like the NFI, this statistic assumes that all latent variables are uncorrelated (null/independence model) and compares the sample covariance matrix with this null model. As with the NFI, values for this statistic range between 0.0 and 1.0 with values closer to 1.0 indicating good fit.

A cut-off criterion of CFI $\geq$ 0.90 was initially advanced however, recent studies have shown that a value greater than 0.90 is needed in order to ensure that misspecified models are not accepted (Hu and Bentler, 1999). From this, a value of CFI $\geq$ 0.95 is presently recognized as indicative of good fit (Hu and Bentler, 1999). Today this index is included in all SEM programs and is one of the most popularly reported fit indices due to being one of the measures least affected by sample size (Fan *et al.,* 1999).

Table 3.8: NFI, TLI, CFI

Model	NFI Delta1	RFI rho1	IFI Delta2	TLI rho2	CFI
Default model	.862	.848	.907	.897	.907
Saturated model	1.000		1.000		1.000
Independence model	.000	.000	.000	.000	.000

A value close to .95 for both the NFI (Normal fit index) and CFI (Comparative fit index) is considered representative of a well-fitting model (Hu & Bentler, 1999). The NFI and CFI values are .862 and .907 respectively which indicates that the model fitted the data well in the sense that the hypothesized model adequately describe the sample data. The RFI (Relative fit index) coefficient values close to .95 indicate superior fit (Hu & Bentler, 1999). The RFI value is .848 indicating good fit. The value of IFI (Incremental index of fit) is .907 which is consistent with that of CFI in reflecting a well-fitting model. Finally, the TLI (Tucker-Lewis index), consistent with the other indices noted here; with values close to .95 indicate good fit. It is observed that TLI is .897 which is acceptable.

Parsimony-Adjusted Measures: Having a nearly saturated, complex model means that the estimation process is dependent on the sample data. This results in a less rigorous theoretical model that paradoxically produces better fit indices (Mulaik *et al.,* 1989; Crowley and Fan, 1997). To overcome this problem, Mulaik *et al.,* (1989) have developed two parsimony of fit indices; the Parsimony Goodness-of-Fit Index (PGFI) and the Parsimonious Normed Fit Index (PNFI).

The PGFI is based upon the GFI by adjusting for loss of degrees of freedom. The PNFI also adjusts for degrees of freedom however it is based on the NFI (Mulaik *et al.,* 1989). Both of these indices seriously penalize for model complexity which results in parsimony fit index values that are considerably lower than other goodness of fit indices. While no threshold levels have been recommended for these indices, Mulaik *et al.,* (1989) do note that it is possible to obtain parsimony fit indices within the .50 region while other goodness of fit indices achieve values over .90 (Mulaik *et al.,* 1989).

The authors strongly recommend the use of parsimony fit indices in tandem with other measures of goodness-of-fit however, because no threshold levels for these statistics have been recommended it has made them more difficult to interpret.

Second forms of parsimony fit index are those that are also known as 'information criteria' indices. Probably the best known of these indices is the Akaike Information Criterion (AIC) or the Consistent Version of AIC (CAIC) which adjusts for sample size (Akaike, 1974). These statistics are generally used when comparing non-nested or non-hierarchical models estimated with the same data and indicates to the researcher which of the models is the most parsimonious. Smaller values suggest a good fitting, parsimonious model however because these indices are not normed to a 0-1 scale it is difficult to suggest a cut-off other than that the model that produces the lowest value is the most superior. It is also worth noting that these statistics need a sample size of 200 to make their use reliable (Diamantopoulos and Siguaw, 2000).

Table 3.9: PRATIO, PNFI, PGFI

Model	PRATIO	PNFI	PCFI
Default model	.902	.778	.818
Saturated model	.000	.000	.000
Independence model	1.000	.000	.000

The above cluster of fit indices relates to the issue of model parsimony. The first fit index PRATIO (Parsimony ratio) is computed relative to the NFI and CFI. A PNFI and PCFI of .778 and .881 respectively fall in the range of expected values (0 to 1).

NCP: The next set of fit statistics provides the NCP (Noncentrality parameter) estimate. From the table given below, it is observed that the hypothesized model yielded a non-centrality parameter of 1390.584. The confidence interval indicates that we can be 90% confident that the population value of the non-centrality parameter lies between 1255.585 and 1533.184.

Table 3.10: NCP

Model	NCP	LO 90	HI 90
Default model	1390.584	1255.585	1533.184
Saturated model	.000	.000	.000
Independence model	14894.131	14490.095	15304.565

RMSEA: RMSEA (Root mean square error of approximation) value less than .05 indicate good fit and values as high as .08 represent reasonable errors of approximation in the population. For the use of confidence intervals to assess the precision of RMSEA estimates, AMOS reports a 90% interval around the RMSEA value. It is observed that RMSEA value for model is .056 (less than 0.08), with 90% confidence interval ranging from .053 to .059. So it can be concluded that the hypothesized model fits the data well.

Table 3.11: RMSEA

Model	RMSEA	LO 90	HI 90	PCLOSE
Default model	.056	.053	.059	.000
Independence model	.175	.173	.177	.000

HOELTER: Hoelter (1983) proposed that a value in excess of 200 is indicative of a model that adequately represents the sample data. Both the 0.5 and .01 CN values for the hypothesized model are greater than 200 (220 and 228 respectively). Interpretation of this finding, indicates that the size of the sample (N= 566) was satisfactory according to Hoelter's benchmark.

Table 3.12: HOELTER

Model	HOELTER .05	HOELTER .01
Default model	220	228
Independence model	34	35

According to the different indices of goodness-of-fit statistics, as per the present study, the hypothesized model passes all the goodness-of-fit statistics. It indicates that the sample data fit the model well in terms of absolute fit measures like CMIN, RMR, RMSEA and ECVI; parsimonious fit measures like PGFI, PNFI, and AIC; and incremental fit measures like TLI, NFI, AGFI and CFI.

Table 3.13 provides the results for each of the fit indices of the CFA Measurement Model. The results from analyzing the model indicate a good fit of all dimensions.

Table 3.13: Model Fit Indices for the CFA

Model Fit Index	***Scores***
Chi Square/Degree of freedom	**2.790**
Goodness-of-fit Index (GFI)	**.961**
Adjusted Goodness-of-fit Index (AGFI)	**.922**
Non-normed fit Index (NNFI)	**.897**
Comparative Fit Index	**.907**
Root Mean Square Error of Approximation (RMSEA)	**.056**

The above results indicate a good fit of the model that was tested. Thus we can say that the results of Confirmatory Factor Analysis were positive. The above values mentioned in the table are considered to be the important, though other researchers sometimes quote many other indices that have been discussed in this chapter.

3.4.2 Hypotheses Based on Demographics

Companies can increase profitability by utilizing market segmentation. An effective market segmentation technique depends on selecting the relevant segmenting bases and descriptors (Wind, 1978). Segmentation variables must be considered in light of their measurability, availability, reliability and ability to uncover the characteristics of each market segment. Kotler (1997) has proposed that consumer markets should be divided according to geographic, demographic, psychographic, and behavioral variables.

Demographics are considered to be the building blocks of market segmentation (Lin, 2002) Variables typically described as demographic are age, gender, marital status, income and education level which provide the basis for segmentation.

Verain *et al.*, (2012) in their review of 133 articles related to food consumers found that in nearly all of the articles they reviewed, demographic variables were included as profiling variables. Gender, age and education were most frequently included as demographic profiling variables. Demographics are an important element in market segmentation. Therefore, marketers who intend to use social media for marketing should understand the demographics of social media users.

Different hypotheses were developed related to consumers' attitude and behavior towards social networking sites and their demographic attributes.
Hypotheses were framed in two parts- Demographics against social relationship variables, and against electronic word of mouth behavior in social networking sites.
All sub hypotheses were tested for significance using appropriate statistical tools.

In order to explore differences in attitude vis-à-vis consumer demographics, the following hypotheses were framed, where 'H_0' refers to the null hypothesis; 'SR' stands for social relationship variables, 'EWOM' stands for electronic word of mouth behavior variables, 'G' stands for gender, 'A' stands for age group, 'I' stands for income, 'E' stands for education, 'O' stands for occupation.

Social relationship variables- 'SC' stands for social capital, 'TS' stands for tie strength, 'AH' stands for attitude homophily, 'BH' stands for background homophily, 'TR' stands for trust, 'II' stands interpersonal influence, 'NI' refers to normative influence.
Electronic word of mouth behavior variables- 'OL' stands for opinion leading/giving, 'OS' stands for opinion seeking, 'OP' refers to opinion passing.

3.4.2.1 Hypotheses based on Gender

1. **H_0G-SR:** Significant differences do not exist in consumers' attitude towards social relationships on social networking sites with respect to their gender.

   Following seven sub hypotheses were developed for seven social relationship variables.

a) **H_0G-SC:** Significant differences do not exist in consumers' attitude towards social capital on social networking sites with respect to their gender.

b) **H_0G-TS:** Significant differences do not exist in consumers' attitude towards tie strength on social networking sites with respect to their gender.

c) **H_0G-AH:** Significant differences do not exist in consumers' attitude towards attitude homophily on social networking sites with respect to their gender.

d) **H_0G-BH:** Significant differences do not exist in consumers' attitude towards background homophily on social networking sites with respect to their gender.

e) **H_0G-TR:** Significant differences do not exist in consumers' attitude towards trust on social networking sites with respect to their gender.

f) **H_0G-NI:** Significant differences do not exist in consumers' attitude towards normative influence on social networking sites with respect to their gender.

g) **H_0G-II:** Significant differences do not exist in consumers' attitude towards informational influence on social networking sites with respect to their gender.

2. **H_0G-EWOM:** Significant differences do not exist in consumers' electronic word of mouth behavior in social networking sites with respect to their gender. Following three sub hypotheses were developed for electronic word of mouth behavior in social networking sites.

a) **H_0G-OL:** Significant differences do not exist in consumers' opinion leading behavior in social networking sites with respect to their gender.

b) **H_0G-OS:** Significant differences do not exist in consumers' opinion seeking behavior in social networking sites with respect to their gender.

c) **H_0G-OP:** Significant differences do not exist in consumers' opinion passing behavior in social networking sites with respect to their gender.

3.4.2.2 Hypotheses based on Age

1. **H_0A-SR:** Significant differences do not exist in consumers' attitude towards social relationships on social networking sites with respect to their age group.

   Following are the seven sub hypotheses.

a) **H_0A-SC:** Significant differences do not exist in consumers' attitude towards social capital on social networking sites with respect to their age group.

b) **H_0A-TS:** Significant differences do not exist in consumers' attitude towards tie strength on social networking sites with respect to their age group.

c) **H_0A-AH:** Significant differences do not exist in consumers' attitude towards attitude homophily on social networking sites with respect to their age group.

d) **H_0A-BH:** Significant differences do not exist in consumers' attitude towards background homophily on social networking sites with respect to their age group.

e) **H_0A-TR:** Significant differences do not exist in consumers' attitude towards trust on social networking sites with respect to their age group.

f) **H_0A-NI:** Significant differences do not exist in consumers' attitude towards normative influence on social networking sites with respect to their age group.

g) **H_0A-II:** Significant differences do not exist in consumers' attitude towards informational influence on social networking sites with respect to their age group.

2. **H_0A-EWOM:** Significant differences do not exist in consumers' electronic word of mouth behavior in social networking sites with respect to their age group.

   Following are the three sub hypotheses.

a) **H_0A-OL:** Significant differences do not exist in consumers' opinion leading behavior in social networking sites with respect to their age group.

b) **H_0A-OS:** Significant differences do not exist in consumers' opinion seeking behavior in social networking sites with respect to their age group.

c) **H_0A-OP:** Significant differences do not exist in consumers' opinion passing behavior in social networking sites with respect to their age group.

3.4.2.3 Hypotheses based on Income

1. **H_0I-SR:** Significant differences do not exist in consumers' attitude towards social relationships on social networking sites with respect to their income.

   Following are the seven sub hypotheses:

a) **H_0I-SC**: Significant differences do not exist in consumers' attitude towards social capital on social networking sites with respect to their income.

b) **H_0I-TS**: Significant differences do not exist in consumers' attitude towards tie strength on social networking sites with respect to their income.

c) **H_0I-AH**: Significant differences do not exist in consumers' attitude towards attitude homophily on social networking sites with respect to their income.

d) **H_0I-BH**: Significant differences do not exist in consumers' attitude towards background homophily on social networking sites with respect to their income.

e) **H_0I-TR**: Significant differences do not exist in consumers' attitude towards trust on social networking sites with respect to their income.

f) **H_0I-NI**: Significant differences do not exist in consumers' attitude towards normative influence on social networking sites with respect to their income.

g) **H0I-II:** Significant differences do not exist in consumers' attitude towards informational influence on social networking sites with respect to their income.

2. **H_0I-EWOM:** Significant differences do not exist in consumers' electronic word of mouth behavior in social networking sites with respect to their income.

Following are three sub hypotheses:

a) **H_0I-OL**: Significant differences do not exist in consumers' opinion leading behavior in social networking sites with respect to their income.

b) **H_0I-OS:** Significant differences do not exist in consumers' opinion seeking behavior in social networking sites with respect to their income.

c) **H_0I-OP:** Significant differences do not exist in consumers' opinion passing behavior in social networking sites with respect to their income.

3.4.2.4 Hypotheses based on Education

1. **H_0E-SR:** Significant differences do not exist in consumers' attitude towards social relationships on social networking sites with respect to their education.

   Following are the seven sub hypotheses.

a) **H_0E-SC:** Significant differences do not exist in consumers' attitude towards social capital on social networking sites with respect to their education.

b) **H_0E-TS:** Significant differences do not exist in consumers' attitude towards tie strength on social networking sites with respect to their education.

c) **H_0E-AH:** Significant differences do not exist in consumers' attitude towards attitude homophily on social networking sites with respect to their education.

d) **H_0E-BH:** Significant differences do not exist in consumers' attitude towards background homophily on social networking sites with respect to their education.

e) **H_0E-TR:** Significant differences do not exist in consumers' attitude towards trust on social networking sites with respect to their education.

f) **H_0E-NI:** Significant differences do not exist in consumers' attitude towards normative influence on social networking sites with respect to their education.

g) **H_0E-II:** Significant differences do not exist in consumers' attitude towards informational influence on social networking sites with respect to their education.

2. **H_0E-EWOM:** Significant differences do not exist in consumers' electronic word of mouth behavior in social networking sites with respect to their education.

   Following are the three sub hypotheses:

a) **H_0I-OL:** Significant differences do not exist in consumers' opinion leading behavior in social networking sites with respect to their education.

b) **H_0I-OS:** Significant differences do not exist in consumers' opinion seeking behavior in social networking sites with respect to their education.

c) **H_0I-OP:** Significant differences do not exist in consumers' opinion passing behavior in social networking sites with respect to their education.

3.4.2.5 Hypotheses based on Occupation

1. **H_0O-SR:** Significant differences do not exist in consumers' attitude towards social relationships on social networking sites with respect to their occupation.

   Following are three seven sub hypotheses:

a) **H_0O-SC:** Significant differences do not exist in consumers' attitude towards social capital on social networking sites with respect to their occupation.

b) **H_0O-TS:** Significant differences do not exist in consumers' attitude towards tie strength on social networking sites with respect to their occupation.

c) **H_0O-AH:** Significant differences do not exist in consumers' attitude towards attitude homophily on social networking sites with respect to their occupation.

d) **H_0O-BH:** Significant differences do not exist in consumers' attitude towards background homophily on social networking sites with respect to their occupation.

e) **H_0O-TR:** Significant differences do not exist in consumers' attitude towards trust on social networking sites with respect to their occupation.

f) **H_0O-NI:** Significant differences do not exist in consumers' attitude towards normative influence on social networking sites with respect to their occupation.

g) **H_0O-II:** Significant differences do not exist in consumers' attitude towards informational influence on social networking sites with respect to their occupation.

2. **H_0O-EWOM:** Significant differences do not exist in consumers' electronic word of mouth behavior in social networking sites with respect to their occupation.

   Following are the three sub hypotheses:

a) **H_0O-OL:** Significant differences do not exist in consumers' opinion leading behavior in social networking sites with respect to their occupation.

b) **H_0O-OS:** Significant differences do not exist in consumers' opinion seeking behavior in social networking sites with respect to their occupation.

c) **H_0O-OP:** Significant differences do not exist in consumers' opinion passing behavior in social networking sites with respect to their occupation.

3.4.3 Hypotheses- Social Relationships and Electronic Word of Mouth Behavior of Consumers in Social Networking Sites

The revolutionary development of social networking sites has provided marketers a new marketing and communications channel, which again indicates that a substantial potential exists for electronic word of mouth research. Several questions are significant in the understanding of electronic word of mouth behavior in social networking sites. For example, do social relationships created and maintained via social networking sites contribute to electronic word of mouth behaviors on these sites? Do individuals with different relations with others exhibit varying levels of engagement for electronic word of mouth in social networking sites? From a consumer behavior perspective, prior research on electronic word of mouth has failed to consider the influence of social factors on electronic word of mouth communications.

Past studies on electronic word of mouth behaviors in marketing and communication research has mainly focused on consequences and outcomes. However, little is known about the potential determinants of consumers' electronic word of mouth behavior in social networking sites. This is particularly crucial in the understanding of electronic word of mouth in social networking sites, as consumers have the potential to reach a large audience rather than merely members in their personal network. All together, this study presents the first investigation of electronic word of mouth in social networking sites by examining the role of social relationship factors in such a phenomenon.

Online social websites have generated a tremendous amount of product-related electronic word of mouth. As such, social networking sites have considerably changed the way that consumers make purchase decisions by allowing consumers to freely interact with other consumers, marketers, and members of their personal networks (Hung and Li, 2007; Niederhoffer *et al.,* 2007). As consumers now have increased opportunities to communicate with each other, understanding social relationships established and maintained on social networking sites is particularly critical to identify potential market influencers and use them for accelerating positive electronic word of mouth.

Current research concerning social relationship factors as antecedents of word of mouth influence (e.g., Wiedmann, Hennigs, and Langner, 2007) has suggested that variables such as social capital (Stephen and Lehmann 2008), tie strength (Brown and Reingen,

1987), demographic similarity and perceptual affinity (Brown and Reingen, 1987; Gilly *et al.,* 1998), trust (Nisbet, 2006), and interpersonal influence (Bearden, Netemeyer, and Teel, 1989) are important drivers that lead to the effectiveness of word of mouth communication. It is argued that these social relationship variables may be applied to influence electronic word of mouth communication in social networking sites.

In this chapter, hypotheses are developed based on a review of relevant literature on social relationship variables. Five hypotheses are proposed to examine the relationships between social relationships and electronic word of mouth communications among social networking site users.

Social Capital

The first social relationship variable that is of concern in this study is social capital.

Social capital describes the pattern and intensity of networks among people and the shared values which arise from those networks. Research has shown that higher levels of social capital are associated with better health, higher educational achievement, better employment outcomes, and lower crime rates.

Formal and informal networks are central to the concept of social capital. They are defined as the personal relationships which are accumulated when people interact with each other in families, workplaces, neighbourhoods, local associations and a range of informal and formal meeting places. Social capital can have an impact on electronic word of mouth behavior on social networks.

In an effort to investigate the influence of social capital on electronic word of mouth communication via social networking sites, the first hypothesis is formulated to examine the role of social capital.

H_0SC-OL: There is no significant impact of social capital on opinion leading behavior on social networking sites.

H_0SC-OS: There is no significant impact of social capital on opinion seeking behavior on social networking sites.

H_0SC-OP: There is no significant impact of social capital on opinion passing behavior on social networking sites.

Tie Strength

With readily available personal networks in social networking sites, consumers' product choices may be influenced by both stable and intimate "strong tie" interactions as well as randomly-connected "weak ties" (e.g., unfamiliar friends of friends).

Although strong ties possess an impact on the individual and small group level, the asynchronous and connective characteristics of social networking sites allow weak ties to facilitate their potential influence by extending consumers' interpersonal networks to external organizations or groups. This accelerates electronic word of mouth communication throughout a large-scale network. Such strong and weak ties developed via social networking sites may stimulate the diffusion of news, rumors, fashions, and more importantly, product-related information, thereby encouraging consumers' engagement in electronic word of mouth behavior. Therefore, the second hypothesis is proposed to explore such phenomena.

H_0TS-OL: There is no significant impact of tie strength on opinion leading behavior on social networking sites.

H_0TS-OS: There is no significant impact of tie strength on opinion seeking behavior on social networking sites.

H_0TS-OP: There is no significant impact of tie strength on opinion passing behavior on social networking sites.

Homophily

Another social relationship variable that could yield valuable insights into the understanding of electronic word of mouth in social networking sites is homophily. In communication research, homophily concerns the degree of similarity between communicators and receivers (Gilly *et al.,* 1998; Rogers and Bhowmik, 1970).

Based on the above discussion, social networking sites may excel in attracting homophilious consumers who have common product interests. This phenomenon increases their likelihood in using homophilious social contacts as a source of product information, and thereby engaging in electronic word of mouth behaviors. Yet different individuals may display distinct social relationships in the same online social venue. Social networking site users are likely to have different perceptions of being similar to or unique from other contacts, and subsequently, exhibit different levels of perceived homophily.

Thus, it is imperative to understand differences in levels of perceived homophily among social networking site users, so as to fully understand the characteristics of electronic word of mouth occurring on these sites. Accordingly, it is anticipated that social networking site users with a higher level of perceived homophily tend to participate in electronic word of mouth via these social venues to a greater extent compared to users with a relatively lower level of perceived homophily.

Based on the inputs from EFA results, homophily was grouped into two different categories- attitude and background homophily. Thus two different set of hypotheses were framed for this construct.

H_0AH-OL: There is no significant impact of attitude homophily on opinion leading behavior on social networking sites.

H_0AH-OS: There is no significant impact of attitude homophily on opinion seeking behavior on social networking sites.

H_0AH-OP: There is no significant impact of attitude homophily on opinion passing behavior on social networking sites.

H_0BH-OL: There is no significant impact of background homophily on opinion leading behavior on social networking sites.

H_0BH-OS: There is no significant impact of background homophily on opinion seeking behavior on social networking sites.

H_0BH-OP: There is no significant impact of background homophily on opinion passing behavior on social networking sites.

Trust in Social Networking Site Contacts

Trust is another social relationship variable that is incorporated in the conceptual discussion in this study to examine how social relationships in social networking sites affect consumers' decisions to participate in electronic word of mouth in these sites.

In the case of social networking sites, consumers may evaluate the value of product information based on the perceived interpersonal factors, such as perceived integrity, expertise, honesty, sincerity, congeniality, and timeliness, all of which are important predictors of trust (Moorman, Deshpande, and Zaltman, 1993). Because users tend to use their real identity in social networking sites, the unique social and interactive nature of this new medium makes offline contacts (e.g., friends and family) available for online information exchange, which increases perceived trust in social networking site contacts.

That is, consumers tend to use information from their existing personal networks in social networking sites that they trust and share common interests and activities. Accordingly, if consumers have high levels of perceived trust with their contacts in social networking sites, this could transfer their decision to pass along or receive product information via the sites. As a result, such trust may facilitate the flow of information in social networking sites and thus increase the likelihood that consumers will consider using electronic word of mouth communication when making a purchase decision.

Along the same line of discussion, trust in social networking site contacts is conceptualized in the context of social relationships. While it is indisputable that trust is a key element in relationship buildings and electronic word of mouth behaviors in social networking sites, the degrees of trust in social networking site contacts may lead to varying extents of users' engagement in electronic word of mouth.

Despite the general understanding of how trust influences electronic word of mouth is limited; degrees of perceived trust may play an essential contributing role in electronic word of mouth behaviors in social networking sites. That is, social networking site users with a higher level of perceived trust in their contacts may engage in electronic word of mouth in social networking sites to a greater extent than users with a lower level of perceived trust. Hence, the following hypothesis is outlined to gauge whether perceived trust in social networking site contacts affect electronic word of mouth communicated via these sites.

H_0TR-OL: There is no significant impact of trust on opinion leading behavior on social networking sites.

H_0TR-OS: There is no significant impact of trust on opinion seeking behavior on social networking sites.

H_0TR-OP: There is no significant impact of trust on opinion passing behavior on social networking sites.

Role of Interpersonal Influence

Consumer susceptibility to interpersonal influence (Bearden, Netemeyer, and Teel, 1989) is another construct that could be applicable to explain the role of social relationships in electronic word of mouth in social networking sites. Because electronic word of mouth focuses on online information exchange among -consumers through social interactions, social norms and interpersonal influences are key determinants of such electronic word of mouth behavior.

Although consumer susceptibility to interpersonal influence has been conceptualized as a two dimensional construct, *normative* and *informational* influence, both influences may drive electronic word of mouth behaviors in social networking sites. However, differences in the degree and pattern of interpersonal influence among individuals may lead to social networking site users' divergent electronic word of mouth behaviors. For instance, individuals who are more susceptible to informational influence focus on the information value of the message transmitted, whereas individuals who are more amenable to normative influences emphasize the process of transmission and relationship buildings (Laroche, Kalamas, and Cleveland, 2005).

As a result, social networking site users who tend to be subject to informational influence are predicted to display a higher need to acquire valuable information from knowledgeable contacts in order to guide their purchases, thereby facilitating their engagement in electronic word of mouth in social networking sites. On the other hand, social networking site users who tend to be susceptible to normative influences are more likely to conform to the expectations of significant contacts and seek social approval through the acquisition and use of the same products and brands. Such behaviors are associated with the influence of electronic word of mouth, where users of social networking sites view their contacts as an important source of product information.

Given this perspective, it is reasonable to argue that consumer's attitude towards both *normative* and *informational* influence will lead to their use of social networking sites as a vehicle for electronic word of mouth. Thus, the fifth hypothesis is put forth to test whether interpersonal influence has an impact on electronic word of mouth in social networking sites. Two different sets of hypotheses were framed, based on EFA results.

H_0NI-OL: There is no significant impact of normative influence on opinion leading behavior on social networking sites.

H_0NI-OS: There is no significant impact of normative influence on opinion seeking behavior on social networking sites.

H_0NI-OP: There is no significant impact of normative influence on opinion passing behavior on social networking sites.

H_0II-OL: There is no significant impact of informational influence on opinion leading behavior on social networking sites.

H_0II-OS: There is no significant impact of informational influence on opinion seeking behavior on social networking sites.

H_0II-OP: There is no significant impact of informational influence on opinion passing behavior on social networking sites.

In summary, the hypotheses concerned the impact of social variables on electronic word of mouth behavior in social networking sites.

Because social networking sites provide interactive and convenient applications (i.e., personal profiles) and established personal networks (i.e., friend lists) for information exchange and sharing, users who tend to have a high frequency of social interactions can easily and quickly disseminate product information and ideas, furthering the development of electronic word of mouth.

As social networking sites have become an essential activity in Internet users' daily life, it is necessary to examine whether social relationships may affect the use of this rapid growth new social medium. Given that social networking site users may have different degrees of engagement in relationship building and brand activities in social networking sites, customized adjustments are required for advertising strategies to make them effective.

This study offers a new theoretical foundation for linking social relationships and electronic word of mouth in social networking sites. Electronic word of mouth is an important online communication phenomenon that exerts a great impact on consumer purchase decisions. Given that relationship building and social engagement are major activities in online social channels, it is expected that social relationships of social networking site users could contribute to different degrees and patterns of electronic word of mouth behavior occurring via these sites.

3.4.4 Techniques of Analysis

First, various descriptive analyses were performed to examine the characteristics of the sample as well as use of social networking sites in general. Means and standard deviations for all measures were also obtained. To test the hypotheses based on demographics, ANOVA and t tests were being performed on the data.

For testing the hypothesized relationships between the predictors and electronic word of mouth behavior variables, SEM (Structural Equation Modeling) was applied on the data. Through the use of SPSS, EFA (Exploratory Factor Analysis) was carried out, which was then followed by CFA (Confirmatory Factor Analysis). CFA was used to confirm the exploratory factor model by determining the goodness of fit between hypothesized model and sample data (to test the hypotheses as to what social relationship factors influence electronic word of mouth behaviors in social networking sites).

3.5 Methodology (Research Design, Research Instrument, Sampling, Methods of Data Collection, Techniques of Analysis) - Company Study

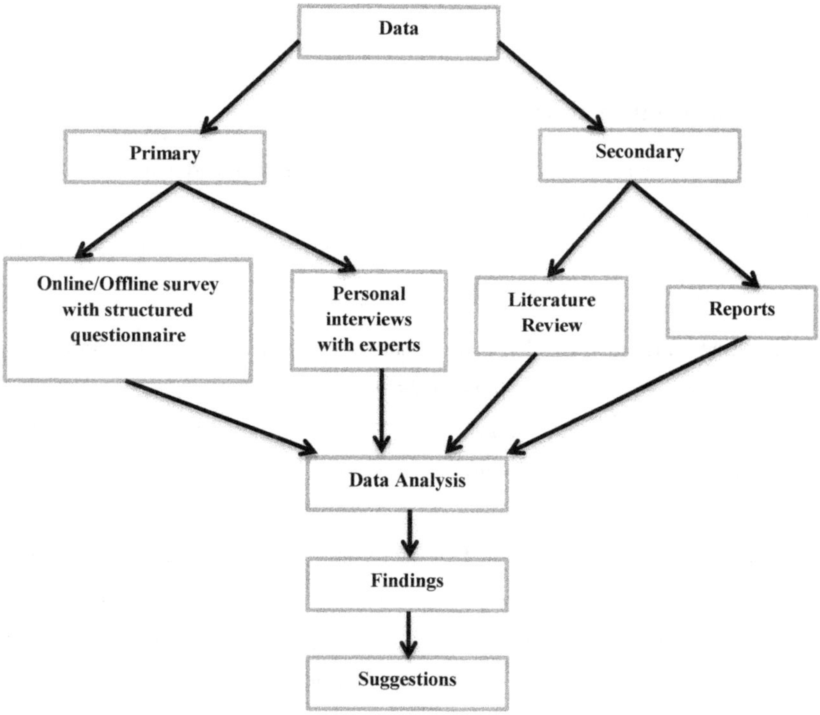

Fig 3.3 Research Design – Company Study ***(Source: Developed by Researcher)***

3.5.1 Research- Company Perspective

A Study of Use of Social Networking Sites as a Marketing Communication Tool, Across Select Sectors

To find out the use of social networking sites in marketing, the purposes of usage within different sectors, and metrics of evaluation to test effectiveness, an empirical study is required.

3.5.1.1 Research Instrument

A comparative study of use of social networking sites as a marketing communication tool, across selected sectors was carried out. Sectors covered in the study were FMCG (Fast Moving Consumer Goods), Automobile, Consumer Electronics/Home Appliances and Banking, Financial Services and Insurance.

The research attempts to understand the nature, and level, of social networking sites' usage by businesses and brands in India; its objectives and measurement.

The research aimed at finding out how social networking sites are used in different organizations with special reference to purposes of usage & metrics/measurement of effectiveness.

In this research, the self-constructed questionnaire was used for conducting the survey. The questionnaire was based on inputs from research taken up by "Strategic social media solutions and NM Incite (Nielsen/ McKinsey Company)" and discussions with few social media experts and digital marketers. Both offline and online methods were used for collecting data.

The purposes, for which social networking sites are used by brand/organizations, were evaluated across sectors. These purposes include: Provide product information/knowledge; Integrate current ad campaign; Two way communication; Speedy redressal of grievances; Faster replies to feedback; Better knowledge of upcoming marketing campaigns; Competitive intelligence; Lead generation; E commerce; Online reputation management or Online PR; Product ideas and development ; Sales promotion (contests, events, etc.); Launch of new products or extensions; Buzz creation; Recruitment; Information about channel or dealerships.

The metrics which the organizations deploy to evaluate success of social networking sites as an effective marketing communication tool, were studied across sectors- Growth in number of participants (users, fans, friends, followers etc. on web or mobile touch points & community); Impact on sentiment and opinion; Volume, quality & cost of lead generated or conversions; E-commerce revenues; Brand awareness; Insights of customers, competition, market; Impact on sales; Support during crisis; Share of voice vis-à-vis agreed competition; Search engine ranking or web traffic; Customer satisfaction score (including net promoter score or recommendations); Co-creation of products & services; Mention & prominence in relevant conversations; Increased engagement scores (retweets, likes, comments).

3.5.1.2 Sampling and Data Collection

The data was collected from companies which have incorporated social media in their marketing communication program.

Desired audience were senior and midlevel managers working in advertising, branding and marketing; professionals in advertising agencies or digital and social media agencies; people involved indirectly in marketing communication in organizations

Judgmental and Convenience sampling methods were used to collect data.
Judgmental sampling is a non-probability sampling technique where the researcher selects units to be sampled based on their knowledge and professional judgment. This type of sampling technique is also known as purposive sampling and authoritative sampling.

Purposive sampling is used in cases where the specialty of an authority can select a more representative sample that can bring more accurate results than by using other probability sampling techniques. The process involves nothing but purposely handpicking individuals from the population based on the authority's or the researcher's knowledge and judgment.
Judgmental sampling design is usually used when a limited number of individuals possess the trait of interest. It is the only viable sampling technique in obtaining information from a very specific group of people. It is also possible to use judgmental sampling if the researcher knows a reliable professional or authority that he thinks is capable of assembling a representative sample.

Around 250 brands/organizations were reached, out of which, 147 responded. 10 responses were found to be incomplete / unsuitable, so the total responses used in the study was 137.

Brands/Organizations covered in study: FMCG: 50, Consumer Electronics/Home Appliances: 30, Automobile: 31, Banks and Financial Services: 26

The basis of choosing these four sectors was to include a mix of products and services in the study. Moreover, these sectors have been spending enormous budget on marketing communication. FMCG spends maximum money on advertising (Brand Equity, Economic Times, June 2014) in India. It is assumed that digital advertising expenses are likely to rise in the next few years.

This study was done across four select sectors, so the sample size was restricted to 137 only.

3.5.2 Hypotheses- A Comparative Analysis of the Use and Evaluation of Social Networking Sites as a Marketing Communication Tool across Select Sectors

The use of social networks as marketing tool is gradually growing, for various advantages they offer to companies, start-ups, etc. In India, the growth of social networks like Facebook and its acceptability amongst people have opened new avenues for the marketers.

The companies use social networks for different reasons based on the companies' strategies and at the same time, have to devise metrics of evaluating use of social networks in marketing.

This study was based on the inputs from a survey report of Blog works and NM Incite, "India Social Media Survey, 2010 Report, Insights from Organisations and Marketers, Blog works – Strategic Social Media Solutions and NM Incite (A Nielsen/ McKinsey Company)"

The study revealed the following trends of social media usage in brands and organizations.

- Brands and organisations are currently in a transition phase, on their journey towards strategic engagement.
- Customers form the largest stakeholder group being targeted using social media.
- Influencers and Media form the other two key stakeholders
- Facebook and Twitter dominate as preferred channels among marketers
- Most brands and organisations have focused on creating presence on third party channels than building own community/ channels.
- Mobile is emerging as an area of strong interest among marketers.
- Social media is still a numbers game, where growth of participants/members/fans defines success than impact on sentiment and opinion and relevance of conversation - There is a stated need for having a social media policy among organisations.
- Budgets are on the rise with marketers planning to spend more on social media in the next two years.

Social media usage varies in different sectors, as per the needs and utility in various companies. There is a need to explore how the planning, implementation or execution, measurement happens in various sectors. These findings will help in comparing the social media strategy amongst various marketing organization, and future road of directions can be planned out.

The present study focussed on the purposes and metrics of evaluation across different sectors in Indian context. The study included a comparative analysis of the use and evaluation of social networking sites as a marketing communication tool across four sectors namely- Fast Moving Consumer Goods, Automobile, Consumer Electronics/Home Appliances and Banking, Financial Services & Insurance.

To find out the differences between the nature and level of usage, purposes and metrics of measurement, across four sectors, the following hypotheses were framed.

$H_0$1: There is no significant difference in use of various forms of marketing communication channels across different sectors.

$H_0$2: There is no significant difference in years of engagement through social media channels across different sectors.

$H_0$3: There is no significant difference in use of various forms of social media channels across different sectors.

$H_0$4: There is no significant difference in budget allotted to social networking sites across different sectors.

$H_0$5: There is no significant difference in frequency of managing social networking sites across different sectors.

$H_0$6: There is no significant difference in the purposes for which social networking sites are used across different sectors.

$H_0$7: There is no significant difference in metrics deployed to evaluate effectiveness of social networking sites, across different sectors.

3.5.3 Techniques of Analysis

To study the organizational differences in all the variables, analysis of variance (ANOVA) was being applied to examine the difference in means. LSD post-hoc comparisons were carried out to confirm where the differences occurred between groups.

When an analysis of variance (ANOVA) gives a significant result, this indicates that at least one group differs from the other groups. Yet, the omnibus test does not indicate which group differs. In order to analyze the pattern of difference between means, ANOVA is often followed by specific comparisons, and the most commonly used involves comparing two means (the so called pairwise comparisons).

The first pairwise comparison technique was developed by Fisher in 1935 and is called the least significant difference (LSD) test. This technique can be used only if the ANOVA F omnibus is significant. The main idea of LSD is to compute the smallest significant difference between two means as if these means had been the only means to be compared (i.e., with a t test) and to declare significant any difference larger than LSD.

Chapter 4

Data Analysis and Interpretation

Chapter Overview

4.1 Preliminary Examination of Data

4.2 Profile of the Respondents

4.3 An Analysis of SNS Users- Based on Involvement in Activities on Social Networking Sites

4.4 Consumers' Attitude towards Social Relationship Variables; and Electronic Word of Mouth in Social Networks, with respect to Demographic Variables

4.5 SEM Results: Social Relationships and Electronic Word of Mouth Behavior of Consumers in Social Networking Sites

4.6 Use of Social Networks within Organizations

Data Analysis and Interpretation

Chapter Overview

In this chapter, a detailed analysis of the data is being carried out. An analysis of the primary data generated by the questionnaire survey is presented. A preliminary examination of the data as well as descriptive analysis is presented in the beginning. The next part describes the profile of the respondents. Thereafter, an analysis is being done to segment social network users into clusters based on activities undertaken on social networking sites.

The next section discusses the findings and interpretation of attitude towards social networking sites with respect to demographic variables. In this section, hypotheses based on demographic variables are tested.

Hypotheses based on social relationships and electronic word of mouth behaviors of consumers in social networking sites are being tested in the next section. This part uses Structural Equation Modeling technique to analyze the data. Lastly, findings and interpretation with respect to use of social networks within organizations, is being discussed.

4.1 Preliminary Examination of Data

The data was analyzed using SPSS 20 and AMOS 20. Screening of the data sets was conducted through an examination of basic descriptive statistics and frequency distribution. Out of 590 voluntary participants, the final sample of 566 respondents was used for data analysis after eliminating incomplete responses and respondents who exhibited extreme and consistent rating patterns.

Descriptive Analysis

Subsequent to data cleaning and screening, a descriptive analysis of data was carried out. Skewness and Kurtosis were obtained to assess normality.

Skewness refers to the symmetry of a distribution, that is, variable whose mean is not in the center of distribution is regarded as skewed variable. On the other hand, kurtosis relates to the peakedness of a distribution. A distribution is said to be normal when the values of the skewness and kurtosis are equal to zero (Malhotra, 2012). Absolute values of univariate skewness indices greater than 3.0 seem to describe extremely skewed data sets and absolute values of kurtosis index greater than 10.0 may suggest a problem and values greater than 20.0 may indicate a more serious one (Hau, 2005). In this study, of all the observed variables, none had skewness greater than 3.00 and none had kurtosis index greater than 6.0. These figures indicate that the data was distributed normally (Refer to Table 4.1).

Table 4.1: Descriptive Statistics- Attitude towards Social Networking Sites

Variables	Mean	S.D.	Variance	Skewness	Kurtosis
Interacting with people on the social networking sites makes me interested in things that happen outside of my town.	3.71	.809	.654	-1.105	1.638
Interacting with people on the social networking sites makes me want to try new things.	3.50	.830	.689	-.577	-.098
Interacting with people on the social networking sites makes me interested in what people different from me are thinking.	3.69	.821	.675	-.869	.818
Talking with people on the social networking sites makes me curious about other places in the world.	3.77	.848	.720	-.796	.724
Interacting with people on the social networking sites makes me feel like part of a larger community.	3.71	.922	.850	-.658	.143
Interacting with people on the social networking sites makes me feel connected to the bigger picture.	3.69	.915	.837	-.574	.029
Interacting with people on the social networking sites reminds me that everyone in the world is connected.	3.88	.856	.733	-.826	.856
Think like me	2.96	.813	.660	-.107	-.385
Behave like me	2.78	.778	.606	.083	-.433
Are similar to me	2.90	.829	.688	.000	-.704
Are from social class similar to mine	3.14	.908	.824	-.229	-.689
Are from economic class like mine	2.95	.865	.748	-.102	-.476
Have status like mine	2.86	.853	.727	.068	-.328
Have moral values like mine	2.86	.859	.738	.118	-.237
The friends on the social networking sites will do everything within their capacity to help others.	2.93	.854	.729	.156	-.359
I trust most of my friends on the social networking sites.	2.99	.931	.867	-.039	-.596
I have confidence in my friends on the social networking sites.	3.10	.857	.735	-.195	-.422
My friends on the social networking sites offer honest opinions.	3.17	.858	.737	-.275	-.224
I can believe in my friends on the social networking sites.	3.13	.863	.745	-.143	-.330
I often persuade my friends on the social networking sites to buy products that I like.	2.40	.981	.962	.362	-.614

My friends on the social networking sites pick their products based on what I have told them.	2.51	.908	.824	.077	-.413
On the social networking sites, I often influence my friends' opinions about products.	2.66	1.000	.999	-.010	-.844
When they choose products, my friends on the social networking sites turn to me for advice.	2.77	1.027	1.054	-.074	-.851
I ask my friends on the social networking sites about what products to buy.	2.79	1.031	1.063	-.092	-.991
I like to get my friends' opinions on the social networking sites before I buy new products.	2.88	1.040	1.081	-.162	-.997
I feel more comfortable choosing products when I have gotten my friends' opinions on them on the social networking sites.	2.96	1.059	1.122	-.170	-.888
I take purchase decisions based on my friends' opinion & experiences.	2.85	.998	.996	-.164	-.629
I tend to pass on information or opinion about the products to my friends on the social networking sites when I find it useful.	3.29	.982	.965	-.693	-.323
When I receive product related information or opinion from a friend, I will pass it along to others on the social networking sites.	3.06	.974	.949	-.263	-.738
I tend to pass along my friends' positive reviews on products to others on the social networking sites.	3.07	.978	.956	-.237	-.647
I tend to pass along my friends' negative reviews on products to others on the social networking sites.	3.07	1.010	1.020	-.232	-.727
I rarely purchase the latest fashion styles until I am sure my friends approve of them.	2.56	.995	.990	.238	-.720
It is important that others like the products and brands I buy.	2.73	1.024	1.048	.048	-.880
When buying products, I generally purchase those brands that I think others will approve of.	2.75	1.020	1.040	-.048	-.923
If other people can see me using a product, I often purchase the brand they expect me to buy.	2.60	.994	.987	.214	-.636
I like to know what brands and products make good impressions on others.	3.08	1.068	1.140	-.301	-.859
I achieve a sense of belonging by purchasing the same products and brands that others purchase.	2.67	.970	.940	.164	-.561
If I want to be like someone, I often try to buy the same brands that they buy.	2.52	1.065	1.135	.323	-.726
If I have little experience with a product, I often ask my friends about the product.	3.44	.999	.997	-.834	-.012
I often consult other people to help choose the best alternative available from a product class.	3.34	1.022	1.045	-.668	-.270
I frequently gather information from friends or family about a product before I buy.	3.42	.986	.973	-.679	-.050
Overall, how important do you feel about your friends on social networking sites	3.27	.844	.712	-.199	.277
Overall, how close do you feel to your friends on social networking sites	3.04	.855	.731	-.149	.153

4.2 Profile of the Respondents

Frequency distribution containing data about gender, age group, annual income, education and occupation were calculated for all the respondents.

The sample comprised of 67% Male (379 respondents) and 33% Female (187 respondents). Most of the participants were in the age group of 21-30 (78.3%). The second prominent group emerged to be 31-40 years with 14.8% respondents falling into this category.

Individual annual income (in lakhs) for respondents was quite varied with maximum respondents (36.2%) earning less than 3 lakhs. The main reason was that 42% percent participants were full time/part time students. Around 25% earned between 3-6 lakhs, 20 % fall into 6-9 lakhs slab, and another 8% in the 9-12 lakhs. Around 11% earned between 9-12 lakhs.

The highest education attained for different respondents were as: Around 68 % were Post Graduates, 6% studied further. The next big category was of Graduates (25%). A major section of respondents (42.2%) were students doing professional courses. Around 54% were in service, working in various disciplines. (Refer to Table 4.2)

Table 4.2 Profile of the Respondents

Gender	**Percentage**	**Frequency(n)**
Male	67.0%	379
Female	33.0%	187
Age (years)	**Percentage**	**Frequency(n)**
Up to 20	1.6%	9
21-30	78.3%	443
31-40	14.8%	84
More than 40	5.3%	30
Individual annual income (in lakhs)	**Percentage**	**Frequency(n)**
Less than 3	36.2%	205
3-6	24.6%	139
6-9	20.5%	116
9-12	7.6%	43
More than 12	11.1%	63

Highest education	Percentage	Frequency(n)
High school	0.7%	4
Graduate	25.3%	143
Postgraduate	67.5%	382
Higher studies	6.0%	34
Any other	0.5%	3
Occupation	**Percentage**	**Frequency(n)**
Student	42.2%	239
Service	53.7%	304
Self employed	3.0%	17
Home maker	0.2%	1
Others: Retired/Not working	0.9%	5

Use of Social Networking Sites in General

Table 4.3: Use of Social Networking Sites on an Average Day (In Hours)

Use of social networking sites on an average day (In hours)	Percentage	Frequency (n)
Less than 1/day	36.6%	207
1-3/day	44.2%	250
3-5/day	12.2%	69
>5/day	7.1%	40

Table 4.4: Use of Different Social Networking Sites

Use of different social networking sites	Mean*	Std. Deviation
Facebook	4.66	.720
Linked In	3.04	1.174
Orkut	1.55	.751
Google+	1.88	1.074
Big Adda	1.09	.388
Flickr	1.21	.584
Blogger	1.37	.800
Hi 5	1.15	.446
My Space	1.11	.423

Table 4.5: Activities on Social Networking Sites

Activities on social networking sites	Mean	Std. Deviation
Updating textual profile information (e.g., status, personal information)	3.13	1.027
Updating visual profile information (e.g., photos, visual background)	3.22	.990
Using applications (e.g., sending virtual gifts, taking quiz, playing games)	2.07	1.065
Reading news feeds, comments on the wall	3.57	.978
Posting comments on the wall	3.41	.958
Searching existing friends	3.25	.988
Making new friends	2.62	1.024
Sending inbox messages	2.92	.959
Chatting (e.g., Facebook chat)	3.34	1.154
Participating in brand communities (e.g., adding brands as friends)	2.30	1.083
Go through featured ads/deals	2.01	.993
Participating in events/contests	1.92	.970

Table 4.6: Topics Discussed with Contacts on Social Networking Sites

Topics discussed with contacts on social networking sites	Percentage	Frequency
Music	46.8%	265
Fashion	21.4%	121
News	55.8%	316
Rumours/Gossip	43.6%	247
Brands	31.3%	177
Political issues	35.0%	198
Social events	52.1%	295
College/Office happenings	69.8%	395
Cinema	52.3%	296
Career options	47.9%	271

The other forms of activities mentioned by respondents were: Sports, philosophy and life's value system, current affairs, poetry, inspirational quotes, express views about some defaming measures against the government, life events, personal interests/hobbies, satirical comments / posts on events of importance, normal updates about who's who and what's with friends, present whereabouts, updates on personal life, catch up with friends, current affairs, simple fun-chat with friends, religious consciousness, jokes, apps, assignments, to pass any message, advertising, various personal events and happenings around, technology, friends' profile updates, nice quotes, friend to friend stuff, personal events in life, looking at family photos, shopping, personal, information and knowledge sharing, educational purpose, you tube clips etc.

In the option "others", many respondents mentioned "sports" as a very popular topic of discussion. Marketers can reach target groups by creating more engaging posts i.e. related to what users indulge in. An example can be sports related activities or posts.

Table 4.7: Respondents' Involvement with Different Categories of Friends

Extent to which respondents are involved with different categories of friends	*Mean	Std. Deviation
Family	2.68	1.113
Relatives	2.74	1.010
Close friends	3.98	.913
Acquaintances	2.98	.919
Class mates	3.72	.955
Neighbours	2.02	.984
Office colleagues	2.91	1.103
People recommended by others	1.81	.877
Unknown people	1.32	.676

Mean calculated on a 5 point scale

Prior to testing the hypotheses, descriptive statistics were run to examine the general use of social networking sites among the respondents. Overall, the descriptive results provided an overview of the usage patterns of social networking sites among users of social networking sites.

Facebook emerged to be the most popular online social networking site (M=4.66, SD= .720), followed by LinkedIn (M=3.04, SD=.720).

When examining the activities in which respondents usually participate while on their favorite social networking site, mean and standard deviation for each item were calculated. The results showed that the top five activities include: reading news feeds and comments on the wall (M = 3.57, SD = .978), posting comments on the wall (M = 3.41, SD = .958), chatting (M = 3.34, SD = 1.154), searching existing friends (M = 3.25, SD = .988), and updating visual profile information (M = 3.22, SD = .990).

Respondents were further asked to indicate the topics they usually talk about with their contacts on the social networking site of their choice. Among the respondents, college/office happenings (69.8%) was the most frequently discussed topic on their social networking site, followed by news (55.8%), cinema (52.3%), social events (52.1.0%), and career options (47.9%).

The extent of involvement of respondents with different categories of friends was highest in close friends (M=3.98, SD= .913) followed by classmates (M=3.72, SD=.955), acquaintances (M=2.98, SD=.919), office colleagues (M=2.91, SD= 1.103).

4.3 Segmentation of Social Network Users

Attitude towards social networking sites vary amongst different kind of people. People tend to behave differently towards usage rate, pattern, activities, involvement, etc. Cluster Analysis was used to segment the users into appropriate categories, which could exhibit similarities in the involvement in various activities.

It is a class of techniques used to classify cases into groups that are relatively homogeneous within themselves and heterogeneous between each other.

Homogeneity (similarity) and heterogeneity (dissimilarity) are measured on the basis of a defined set of variables. These groups are called clusters.

Cluster analysis is especially useful for market segmentation. Segmenting a market means dividing its potential consumers into separate sub-sets where consumers in the same group are similar with respect to a given set of characteristics. Consumers belonging to different groups are dissimilar with respect to the same set of characteristics. This allows one to calibrate the marketing mix differently according to the target consumer group.

Clustering of similar brands or products according to their characteristics allow one to identify competitors, potential market opportunities and available niches.

Cluster analysis allows reducing the number of observations, by grouping them into homogeneous clusters. Thus it helps in data reduction.

A hierarchical method was used to define the number of clusters. Then k-means procedure was used to actually form the clusters. By applying Hierarchical Analysis, three clusters were formed.

Table 4.8: Social Network Users' Involvement in Activities on Social Networking Sites

Activities on Social Networking Sites	Group		
	1	2	3
Updating textual profile information (e.g. status, personal information)	To a very little extent	To a great extent	To some extent
Updating visual profile information (e.g. photos, visual background)	To a very little extent	To a great extent	To some extent
Using applications (e.g. sending virtual gifts, taking quiz, playing games)	Not at all	To some extent	To a very little extent
Reading news feeds, comments on the wall	To some extent	To a great extent	To a great extent
Posting comments on the wall	To some extent	To a great extent	To a great extent
Searching existing friends	To a very little extent	To a great extent	To some extent
Making new friends	To a very little extent	To some extent	To some extent
Sending inbox messages	To a very little extent	To some extent	To some extent
Chatting (e.g., Facebook chat)	To a very little extent	To a great extent	To a great extent
Participating in brand communities	Not at all	To some extent	To a very little extent
Go through featured ads/deals	Not at all	To some extent	To a very little extent
Participating in events/contests	Not at all	To some extent	To a very little extent

(Measurement scale-Likert Scale from 1= Not at all to 5= To a very large extent)

Brandtzaeg and Heim (2011), categorized users by two criteria – how active are users (low activity-high activity) and what is the purpose of using social networking sites (informational or recreational). This approach created 5 categories.

This categorization has been explained in the published research work: Petter Bae Brandtzæg (2012), "Social Networking Sites: Their Users and Social Implications- A Longitudinal Study", *Journal of Computer-Mediated Communication*, 17(4), 467–488.

Further many other researchers have included the same categorization in their studies.

Table 4.9: Brandtzaeg and Heim (2011) Categorization of Social Network Users

Category	Criteria
Sporadics	The 'sporadics' are so named because they visit the community only from time to time, but not on a frequent basis. These users have a low level of participation and tend more toward an informational mode.
Lurkers	Lurkers make up the largest user category. They are named 'lurkers' since they are quite low in participation and participate in activities that are more related to recreation.
Socializers	Their behavior is characterized by recreational in terms of 'small talk' with others, but the users' participation level is high. They score high on 'write letters or messages', 'contact others', and 'look for a new friend'.
Debaters	Debaters are as high as socializers in terms of participation level, characterized by being highly involved in discussions, reading, and writing contributions in general.
Actives	'Actives' are so labeled because these users are engaged in almost all kinds of participation activities within the community, which includes being a member to "publish and share pictures".

Group Characteristics

Group 1: This set of respondents mostly are passive users of social networking sites, as they are not much involved in activities, but have mere social presence. Around 30.5% of the respondents fall into this cluster.

They are completely away from activities like participating in brand communities (e.g. adding brands as friends), going through featured ads/deals , participating in events or contests; and use of applications (e.g. sending virtual gifts, taking quiz, playing games).

To a very little extent, they are involved in updating textual profile information (e.g. status, personal information), updating visual profile information (e.g. photos, visual background), searching existing friends, and making new friends, as well as, sending inbox messages and chatting (e.g. Facebook chat).

To some extent, social network users are engaged in reading news feeds and comments on the wall and posting comments on the wall.

Based on "Brandtzaeg and Heim (2011) categorization of social network users", this group shares the characteristics of "SPORADICS" and "LURKERS".

Group 2: Users in this cluster are fond of updating textual profile information and visual profile information. Reading news feeds and comments on the wall, posting comments on the wall, searching existing friends and chatting online, are important activities, users are engaged with.

This set of social network users are engaged with following activities on a moderate level- Using applications (like sending virtual gifts, taking quiz, playing games), making new friends, sending inbox messages, participating in brand communities (like adding brands as friends), going through featured ads/deals and participating in events/contests.
Overall, this set of users seems to be actively participating in maximum activities on social networks. Around 30% of the users fall into this category.
This group exhibits the characteristics of the group "ACTIVES".

Group 3: To a great extent, users are involved in activities like reading news feeds and others' comments on the wall, posting comments on the wall and chatting. Maximum respondents (40%) fall into this category.

Updating textual profile information like status, personal information; updating visual profile information like photos, visual background, searching existing friends and making new friends and sending inbox messages, are certain activities, which users moderately get involved with.
Using applications like sending virtual gifts, taking quiz, playing games; participating in brand communities like adding brands as friends; going through featured ads and deals; participating in events/contests, are still not very popular activities for engaging in social networks.
The users falling into this category share the characteristics of "SOCIALIZERS" and "DEBATERS".

Table 4.10: ANOVA Table for Cluster Analysis

Activities on Social Networking Sites	F	Sig.
Updating textual profile information (e.g., status, personal information)	134.158	.000
Updating visual profile information (e.g., photos, visual background)	141.054	.000
Using applications (e.g., sending virtual gifts, taking quiz, playing games)	138.822	.000
Reading news feeds, comments on the wall	59.341	.000
Posting comments on the wall	176.925	.000
Searching existing friends	120.237	.000
Making new friends	73.199	.000
Sending inbox messages	87.899	.000
Chatting (e.g., Facebook chat)	157.500	.000
Participating in brand communities (e.g., adding brands as friends)	226.780	.000
Go through featured ads/deals	224.033	.000
Participating in events/contests	249.577	.000

The ANOVA table tells that which of the twelve variables is significantly different across the 3 groups. Based on the assumption that ANOVA is a valid test, the interpretation of clusters and difference across clusters were made on the basis of those variables, which were significant across clusters at 0.05 level. The last column in ANOVA table indicates that all variables are significant at 0.05 level, as they have probability values less than 0.05.

4.4 Consumers' Attitude towards Social Relationship Variables; and Electronic Word of Mouth in Social Networks, with respect to Demographic Variables

4.4.1 Variations in Consumers' Attitude towards Social Relationships on Social Networks with respect to Gender

Gender as a demographic variable is the one whose influence on the consumers' attitude and behavior has been most often studied. Over the last decade, it has been widely accepted within gender and technology studies that technology and gender is co-constructed, which means that they are mutually constitutive (Wajcman, 2004). The notion of mutual constitution recognizes not only that technology and gender are socially constructed, but that each plays a significant role within the construction of the other.

This part of the analysis describes the variations in consumers' attitude towards social relationships on social networks based on gender.

4.4.1.1 Variation in Consumers' Attitude towards Social Capital on Social Networks with respect to Gender

The table 4.11 shows the descriptives and the results of 't' test for consumers' attitude towards social capital on social networks with respect to gender. The mean values acquired by male and female is 3.72 and 3.67 respectively, which inclines towards higher mean value on a five point scale.

Table 4.11: Variation in Consumers' Attitude towards Social Capital on Social Networks with respect to Gender

Gender	N	Mean	S. D.	t- value	Sig.	Remark
Male	379	3.72	.568	.873	.383	Not Significant
Female	187	3.67	.650			

The results of 't' test as shown above shows that significant difference do not exist for consumers' attitude towards social capital on social networks with respect to gender (t=.873, sig. = .383). Since the associated probability is less than the significance level of 0.05, the null hypothesis *"**H_0G-SC:** Significant differences do not exist in consumers' attitude towards social capital on social networking sites with respect to their gender"* is supported.

Social capital emerged as a significant predictor of electronic word of mouth behavior (as explained later). We can conclude that gender classification will not make any sense if the attitude towards social capital is to be measured.

4.4.1.2 Variation in Consumers' Attitude towards Tie Strength on Social Networks with respect to Gender

The table 4.12 shows the descriptives and the results of 't' test for consumers' attitude towards tie strength on social networks with respect to gender. The mean values acquired by male and female is 3.21 and 3.05 respectively, which is moderately placed on a five point scale.

Table 4.12: Variation in Consumers' Attitude towards Tie Strength on Social Networks with respect to Gender

Gender	N	Mean	S. D.	t- value	Sig.	Remark
Male	379	3.21	.810	2.282	.023	**Significant**
Female	187	3.05	.744			

The results of 't' test as shown above shows that significant difference exists for consumers' attitude towards tie strength on social networks with respect to gender (t=2.282, sig. = .023). Since the associated probability is less than the significance level of 0.05, the null hypothesis *"**H_0G-TS:** Significant differences do not exist in consumers' attitude towards tie strength on social networking sites with respect to their gender"* is not supported.

It can be seen from the above table, that the mean value for males (3.21) is significantly higher than that of females (3.05). It may be presumed, that males are more open to accepting requests from weak ties, even unknown people. As per the socio-cultural norms followed in India, many females tend to maintain privacy.

4.4.1.3 Variation in Consumers' Attitude towards Attitude Homophily on Social Networks with respect to Gender

The table 4.13 shows the descriptives and the results of 't' test for consumers' attitude towards attitude homophily on social networks with respect to gender. The mean values acquired by male and female is 2.90 and 2.84 respectively.

Table 4.13: Variation in Consumers' Attitude towards Attitude Homophily on Social Networks with respect to Gender

Gender	N	Mean	S. D.	t- value	Sig.	Remark
Male	379	2.90	.724	.905	.366	**Not Significant**
Female	187	2.84	.654			

The results of 't' test as shown above shows that significant difference do not exist for consumers' attitude towards attitude homophily on social networks with respect to gender (t=.905, sig. = .366). Since the associated probability is more than the significance level of 0.05, the null hypothesis *"**H_0G-AH:** Significant differences do not exist in consumers' attitude towards attitude homophily on social networking sites with respect to their gender"* stands supported.

4.4.1.4 Variation in Consumers' Attitude towards Background Homophily on Social Networks with respect to Gender

The table 4.14 shows the descriptives and the results of 't' test for consumers' attitude towards background homophily on social networks with respect to gender. The mean values acquired by male and female is 2.99 and 2.88 respectively.

Table 4.14: Variation in Consumers' Attitude towards Background Homophily on Social Networks with respect to Gender

Gender	N	Mean	S. D.	t- value	Sig.	Remark
Male	379	2.99	.722	1.862	.063	**Not Significant**
Female	187	2.88	.651			

The results of 't' test as shown above shows that significant difference do not exist for consumers' attitude towards background homophily on social networks with respect to gender (t=1.862, sig. = .063). Since the associated probability is more than the significance level of 0.05, the null hypothesis *"H_0G-BH: Significant differences do not exist in consumers' attitude towards background homophily on social networking sites with respect to their gender"* is supported.

4.4.1.5 Variation in Consumers' Attitude towards Trust on Social Networks with respect to Gender

The table 4.15 shows the descriptives and the results of 't' test for consumers' attitude towards trust on social networks with respect to gender. The mean values acquired by male (3.15) are more than that of female (2.88).

Table 4.15: Variation in Consumers' Attitude towards Trust on Social Networks w.r.t Gender

Gender	N	Mean	S. D.	t- value	Sig.	Remark
Male	379	3.15	.724	4.111	.000	**Significant**
Female	187	2.88	.706			

The results of 't' test as shown above shows that significant difference exists for consumers' attitude towards trust on social networks with respect to gender (t=4.111, sig. = .000). Since the associated probability is less than the significance level of 0.05, the null hypothesis *"H_0G-TR: Significant differences do not exist in consumers' attitude towards trust on social networking sites with respect to their gender"* is not supported.

As males are more open on social networks, their number of contact on social networks are higher too. The mean value for males (3.15) is higher than that of females (2.88). Due to more openness and interactions with their contacts on social networks, males tend to be more responsive to trust factors.

4.4.1.6 Variation in Consumers' Attitude towards Normative Influence on Social Networks with respect to Gender

The table 4.16 shows the descriptives and the results of 't' test for consumers' attitude towards normative influence on social networks with respect to gender. The mean values acquired by male (2.77) and female (2.54) are on a moderate side.

Table 4.16: Variation in Consumers' Attitude towards Normative Influence on Social Networks with respect to Gender

Gender	N	Mean	S. D.	t- value	Sig.	Remark
Male	379	2.77	.813	3.315	.001	**Significant**
Female	187	2.54	.788			

The results of 't' test as shown above shows that significant difference exists for consumers' attitude towards normative influence on social networks with respect to gender (t=3.315, sig. = .001). Since the associated probability is less than the significance level of 0.05, the null hypothesis "***H_0G-NI:*** *Significant differences do not exist in consumers' attitude towards normative influence on social networking sites with respect to their gender"* is not supported.

4.4.1.7 Variation in Consumers' Attitude towards Informational Influence on Social Networks with respect to Gender

The table 4.17 shows the descriptives and the results of 't' test for consumers' attitude towards informational influence on social networks with respect to gender. The mean values acquired by male (3.43) and female (3.33) are on a higher side of five point scale.

Table 4.17: Variation in Consumers' Attitude towards Informational Influence on Social Networks with respect to Gender

Gender	N	Mean	S. D.	t- value	Sig.	Remark
Male	379	3.43	.913	1.210	.227	**Not Significant**
Female	187	3.33	.885			

The results of 't' test as shown above shows that significant difference do not exist for consumers' attitude towards informational influence on social networks with respect to gender (t=1.210, sig. = .227). Since the associated probability is more than the significance level of 0.05, the null hypothesis *"H_0G-II: Significant differences do not exist in consumers' attitude towards informational influence on social networking sites with respect to their gender"* is supported.

Table 4.18: Summary of Hypotheses Testing Results based on Consumers' Attitude towards Social Relationships on Social Networks with respect to Gender

	Hypotheses	**Result**
H_0G-SC	Significant differences do not exist in consumers' attitude towards social capital on social networking sites with respect to their gender.	**Supported**
H_0G-TS	Significant differences do not exist in consumers' attitude towards tie strength on social networking sites with respect to their gender.	**Not Supported**
H_0G-AH	Significant differences do not exist in consumers' attitude towards attitude homophily on social networking sites with respect to their gender.	**Supported**
H_0G-BH	Significant differences do not exist in consumers' attitude towards background homophily on social networking sites with respect to their gender.	**Supported**
H_0G-TR	Significant differences do not exist in consumers' attitude towards trust on social networking sites with respect to their gender.	**Not Supported**
H_0G-NI	Significant differences do not exist in consumers' attitude towards normative influence on social networking sites with respect to their gender.	**Not Supported**
H_0G-II	Significant differences do not exist in consumers' attitude towards informational influence on social networking sites with respect to their gender.	**Supported**

Based on the above results, four sub hypotheses are supported and three sub hypotheses are not supported. This result implies that, the main hypothesis *"H_0G-SR: Significant differences do not exist in consumers' attitude towards social relationships on social networking sites with respect to their gender"*, is weakly supported. So, gender separation is not the solution because it is an unwarranted duplication, which has a huge economic cost.

Table 4.19: Summary of Mean Values of All Dimensions of Social Relationships with respect to Gender

	Social Capital	Tie Strength	Attitude Homophily	Background Homophily	Trust	Normative Influence	Informational Influence
Male	3.72	3.21	2.90	2.99	3.15	2.77	3.43
Female	3.67	3.05	2.84	2.88	2.88	2.54	3.33

As per table 4.19, the mean values amongst males, across all dimensions are higher than the values calculated for the female respondents. This results into a conclusion that males have more positive attitude than females and are more responsive towards social relationship factors. The highest mean value (3.72) is acquired by males for social capital.

Moreover, males show more openness towards use of social networks than their female counterparts, inspired by the social norms existing in the Indian society.

4.4.2 Variations in Consumer Attitude towards Electronic Word of Mouth in Social Networks, with respect to Gender

4.4.2.1 Variations in Consumer Attitude towards Opinion Leading Behavior in Social Networks, with respect to Gender

The table 4.20 shows the descriptives and the results of t' test for attitude towards opinion leading behavior in social networks with respect to gender. The mean values, 2.68 and 2.40 acquired by males and females respectively, show a moderate attitude towards opinion leading behavior.

Table 4.20: Consumer Attitude towards Opinion Leading Behavior in Social Networks with respect to Gender

Gender	N	Mean	S. D.	t- value	Sig.	Remark
Male	379	2.68	.863	3.673	.000	Significant
Female	187	2.40	.825			

The results of 't' test as shown above shows that significant difference exists for attitude towards opinion leading behavior in social networks with respect to gender (t=3.673, sig. = .000). Since the associated probability is less than the significance level of 0.05, the null hypothesis *"H_0G-OL: Significant differences do not exist in consumers' opinion leading behavior in social networking sites with respect to their gender"* is not supported.

The kind of purchases are triggered by the electronic word of mouth communication may differ in case of various product categories. Males have a different choice of products than that of females. Moreover the leadership behavior may vary in both the genders. The persuasion and influencing behavior might be different in case of both the genders.

4.4.2.2 Variations in Consumer Attitude towards Opinion Seeking Behavior in Social Networks, with respect to Gender

The table 4.21 shows the descriptives and the results of 't' test for attitude towards opinion seeking behavior in social networks with respect to gender. The mean values, 2.92 and 2.75 acquired by males and females respectively, show a moderate attitude and behavior towards opinion seeking behavior.

Table 4.21: Consumer Attitude towards Opinion Seeking Behavior in Social Networks with respect to Gender

Gender	N	Mean	S. D.	t- value	Sig.	Remark
Male	379	2.92	.896	2.109	.036	**Significant**
Female	187	2.75	.879			

The results of 't' test as shown above shows that significant difference exists for attitude towards opinion seeking behavior in social networks with respect to gender ($t=2.109$, sig. = .036). Since the associated probability is less than the significance level of 0.05, the null hypothesis *"H_0G-OS: Significant differences do not exist in consumers' opinion seeking behavior in social networking sites with respect to their gender"* is not supported.

Opinion seeking behavior might vary in males and females, as the idea of seeking opinions and views online is related to more openness and interactivity on social networks. Gender differences can be observed in opinion seeking behavior.

4.4.2.3 Variations in Consumer Attitude towards Opinion Passing Behavior in Social Networks, with respect to Gender

The table 4.22 shows the descriptives and the results of 't' test for attitude towards opinion passing behavior in social networks with respect to gender. The mean values, 3.15 and 3.06 acquired by males and females respectively, show a fair attitude towards opinion passing behavior.

Table 4.22: Consumer Attitude towards Opinion Passing Behavior in Social Networks with respect to Gender

Gender	N	Mean	S. D.	t- value	Sig.	Remark
Male	379	3.15	.857	1.080	.281	Not Significant
Female	187	3.06	.900			

The results of 't' test as shown above shows that significant difference do not exist for attitude towards opinion passing behavior in social networks with respect to gender (t=1.080, sig. = .281). Since the associated probability is more than the significance level of 0.05, the null hypothesis *"H_0G-OP: Significant differences do not exist in consumers' opinion passing behavior in social networking sites with respect to their gender"* is supported.

Table 4.23: Summary of Hypotheses Testing Results based on Consumer Attitude towards Electronic Word of Mouth in Social Networks, with respect to Gender

	Hypotheses	Result
H_0G-OL	Significant differences do not exist in consumers' opinion leading behavior in social networking sites with respect to their gender.	Not Supported
H_0G-OS	Significant differences do not exist in consumers' opinion seeking behavior in social networking sites with respect to their gender.	Not Supported
H_0G-OP	Significant differences do not exist in consumers' opinion passing behavior in social networking sites with respect to their gender.	Supported

Based on the above results, one sub hypothesis is supported and two sub hypotheses are not supported. This result implies that, the main hypothesis *"**H_0G-EWOM:** Significant differences do not exist in consumers' electronic word of mouth behavior in social networking sites with respect to their gender"*, is not supported.

Social networking sites provide consumers with opportunities to efficiently create and maintain their personal networks, and both the genders have become open to it. Though, in this study, significant differences in electronic word of mouth behavior were observed between males and females.

Table 4.24: Summary of Mean Values of Electronic Word of Mouth Behavior

Gender/Electronic word of mouth	Opinion Leading	Opinion Seeking	Opinion Passing
Male	2.68	2.92	3.15
Female	2.40	2.75	3.06

As per table 4.24, the mean values amongst males, across all dimensions are high than the values calculated for the female respondents. This results into a conclusion that males have more favorable attitude towards electronic word of mouth in social networking sites. The highest mean value (3.15) is acquired by males for opinion passing behavior.

4.4.3 Variations in Consumers' Attitude towards Social Relationships on Social Networks with respect to Age Groups

Social networking sites have been very popular with young adults aged 18-29 almost since their inception. A national research study by Pew Internet (Madden & Zickuhr, 2011) found that over eight in ten internet users ages 18-29 use social networking sites compared with seven in ten 30-49 year olds, half of 50-64 year olds, and one-third of those age 65 and older.

Similarly, Hampton, Goulet, Rainie & Purcell (2011) found that the 18-35 age grouping made up 48% of social networking site users.

A study done by Charnigo and Barnett-Ellis (2007) indicates that the use of social networking sites increases as age decreases.

4.4.3.1 Variation in Consumers' Attitude towards Social Capital on Social Networks with respect to Age Group

The table 4.25 shows the descriptives and ANOVA results for consumers' attitude towards social capital on social networks with respect to age group.

The mean values of social capital amongst age groups 21-30, 31-40 and more than 40 are somewhat similar, exhibiting values of 3.71, 3.73, and 3.71, respectively

Table 4.25: Variation in Consumers' Attitude towards Social Capital on Social Networks with respect to Age Group

Age Group	N	Mean	Std. Deviation	F	Sig.	Remark
Up to 20	9	3.20	.792			
21-30	443	3.71	.573			
31-40	84	3.73	.651	2.188	.088	Not Significant
More than 40	30	3.71	.675			
Total	566	3.70	.597			

ANOVA shows that there is no significant difference in consumers' attitude towards social capital on social networks with respect to age group. Since the associated probability is more than the significance level of 0.05 (F= 2.188, sig. = .088), the null hypothesis *"H_0A-SC: Significant differences do not exist in consumers' attitude towards social capital on social networking sites with respect to their age group"* is supported.

The mean values of the respondents across various age groups show positive attitude towards social capital. The overall mean value is 3.70, which indicates that a positive attitude exists across age groups.

4.4.3.2 Variation in Consumers' Attitude towards Tie Strength on Social Networks with respect to Age Group

The table 4.26 shows the descriptives and ANOVA results for consumers' attitude towards tie strength on social networks with respect to age group.

The mean values of tie strength amongst age groups 21-30 and 31-40 are 3.15 and 3.29, which shows a positive consumer response towards tie strength.

Table 4.26: Variation in Consumers' attitude towards Tie Strength on Social Networks with respect to Age Group

Age Group	N	Mean	Std. Deviation	F	Sig.	Remark
Up to 20	9	2.77	1.003	**2.793**	**.040**	**Significant**
21-30	443	3.15	.754			
31-40	84	3.29	.912			
More than 40	30	2.88	.837			
Total	566	3.15	.791			

ANOVA shows that there is a significant difference in consumers' attitude towards tie strength on social networks with respect to age group. Since the associated probability is less than the significance level of 0.05 (F= 2.793, sig. = .040), the null hypothesis *"**H_0A-TS:** Significant differences do not exist in consumers' attitude towards tie strength on social networking sites with respect to their age group"* is not supported.

The overall mean value is 3.15, which indicates that somewhat positive attitude exists across age groups.

4.4.3.3 Variation in Consumers' Attitude towards Attitude Homophily on Social Networks with respect to Age Group

The table 4.27 shows the descriptives and ANOVA results for consumers' attitude towards attitude homophily on social networks with respect to age group.

The mean values of tie strength amongst age groups up to 20, 21-30 and more than 40 have values between 2.5 and 3; hence they exhibit a moderate consumer response towards attitude homophily.

Table 4.27: Variation in Consumers' Attitude towards Attitude Homophily on Social Networks with respect to Age Group

Age Group	N	Mean	Std. Deviation	F	Sig.	Remark
Up to 20	9	2.51	.818	**2.551**	**.055**	**Not Significant**
21-30	443	2.87	.690			
31-40	84	3.01	.702			
More than 40	30	2.68	.762			
Total	566	2.88	.701			

ANOVA shows that there is no significant difference in consumers' attitude towards attitude homophily on social networks with respect to age group. Since the associated probability is more than the significance level of 0.05 (F= 2.551, sig. = .055), the null hypothesis *"H_0**A-AH:** Significant differences do not exist in consumers' attitude towards attitude homophily on social networking sites with respect to their age group"* is supported. The overall mean value is 2.88, which indicates that a moderate positive attitude exists across all age groups.

4.4.3.4 Variation in Consumers' Attitude towards Background Homophily on Social Networks with respect to Age Group

The table 4.28 shows the descriptives and ANOVA results for consumers' attitude towards background homophily on social networks with respect to age group.

The mean values of background homophily amongst age groups up to 20, 21-30 and more than 40 have values between 2.5 and 3; hence they exhibit a moderate consumer response towards background homophily.

Table 4.28: Variation in Consumers' Attitude towards Background Homophily on Social Networks with respect to Age Group

Age Group	N	Mean	Std. Deviation	F	Sig.	Remark
Up to 20	9	2.58	.943	**3.067**	**.028**	**Significant**
21-30	443	2.92	.697			
31-40	84	3.13	.665			
More than 40	30	2.93	.688			
Total	566	2.95	.700			

ANOVA shows that there is a significant difference in consumers' attitude towards background homophily on social networks with respect to age group. Since the associated probability is less than the significance level of 0.05 (F= 3.067, sig. = .028), the null hypothesis *"H_0A -BH: Significant differences do not exist in consumers' attitude towards background homophily on social networking sites with respect to their age group"* is not supported.

The overall mean value is 2.95, which indicates that moderate attitude exists across most age groups.

4.4.3.5 Variation in Consumers' Attitude towards Trust on Social Networks with respect to Age Group

The table 4.29 shows the descriptives and ANOVA results for consumers' attitude towards trust on social networks with respect to age group.

The mean values of trust amongst age groups 21-30, 31-40 and more than 40 have values 3.02, 3.25 and 3.24 respectively, hence they exhibit a positive consumer response towards trust.

Table 4.29: Variation in Consumers' Attitude towards Trust on Social Networks with respect to Age Group

Age Group	N	Mean	Std. Deviation	F	Sig.	Remark
Up to 20	9	2.73	.774	**3.651**	**.013**	**Significant**
21-30	443	3.02	.715			
31-40	84	3.25	.751			
More than 40	30	3.24	.732			
Total	566	3.06	.728			

ANOVA shows that there is a significant difference in consumers' attitude towards trust on social networks with respect to age group. Since the associated probability is less than the significance level of 0.05 (F= 3.651, sig. = .013), the null hypothesis *"H_0A-TR: Significant differences do not exist in consumers' attitude towards trust on social networking sites with respect to their age group"* is not supported.

The overall mean value is 3.06, which indicates somewhat positive attitude across most age groups.

4.4.3.6 Variation in Consumers' Attitude towards Normative Influence on Social Networks with respect to Age Group

The table 4.30 shows the descriptives and ANOVA results for consumers' attitude towards trust on social networks with respect to age group.

The mean values amongst all age groups are less than 3; hence they exhibit a moderate consumer response towards normative influence.

Table 4.30: Variation in Consumers' Attitude towards Normative Influence on Social Networks with respect to Age Group

Age Group	N	Mean	Std. Deviation	F	Sig.	Remark
Up to 20	9	2.46	.775	**2.647**	**.048**	**Significant**
21-30	443	2.73	.786			
31-40	84	2.65	.879			
More than 40	30	2.34	.922			
Total	566	2.70	.812			

ANOVA shows that there is a significant difference in consumers' attitude towards normative influence on social networks with respect to age groups. Since the associated probability is less than the significance level of 0.05 (F= 2.647, sig. = .048), the null hypothesis *"H_0A-NI: Significant differences do not exist in consumers' attitude towards normative influence on social networking sites with respect to their age group"* is not supported.

The overall mean value is 2.70, which indicates a moderate attitude across most age groups.

4.4.3.7 Variation in Consumers' Attitude towards Informational Influence on Social Networks with respect to Age Group

The table 4.31 shows the descriptives and ANOVA results for consumers' attitude towards informational influence on social networks with respect to age group.

The mean values amongst age groups- up to 20, 21-30, 31-40 are 3.00, 3.53, and 3.04 respectively; hence they exhibit somewhat positive consumer response towards informational influence.

Table 4.31: Variation in Consumers' Attitude towards Informational Influence on Social Networks with respect to Age Group

Age Group	N	Mean	Std. Deviation	F	Sig.	Remark
Up to 20	9	3.00	1.040	**15.171**	**.000**	**Significant**
21-30	443	3.52	.803			
31-40	84	3.04	1.028			
More than 40	30	2.66	1.253			
Total	566	3.39	.904			

ANOVA shows that there is a significant difference in consumers' attitude towards informational influence on social networks with respect to age groups. Since the associated probability is less than the significance level of 0.05 (F= 15.171, sig. = .000), the null hypothesis *"**H_0A-II:** Significant differences do not exist in consumers' attitude towards informational influence on social networking sites with respect to their age group"* is not supported. The overall mean value is 3.39, which indicates a positive attitude across most age groups.

Table 4.32: Summary of Hypotheses Testing Results based on Consumers' Attitude towards Social Relationships on Social Networks with respect to Age Group

	Hypotheses	Result
H_0A-SC	Significant differences do not exist in consumers' attitude towards social capital on social networking sites with respect to their age group.	**Supported**
H_0A-TS	Significant differences do not exist in consumers' attitude towards tie strength on social networking sites with respect to their age group.	**Not Supported**
H_0A-AH	Significant differences do not exist in consumers' attitude towards attitude homophily on social networking sites with respect to their age group.	**Supported**
H_0A-BH	Significant differences do not exist in consumers' attitude towards background homophily on social networking sites with respect to their age group.	**Not Supported**
H_0A-TR	Significant differences do not exist in consumers' attitude towards trust on social networking sites with respect to their age group.	**Not Supported**
H_0A-NI	Significant differences do not exist in consumers' attitude towards normative influence on social networking sites with respect to their age group.	**Not Supported**
H_0A-II	Significant differences do not exist in consumers' attitude towards informational influence on social networking sites with respect to their age group.	**Not Supported**

Based on the above results, only two sub hypotheses out of total of seven are supported and the remaining five sub hypotheses are not supported. This result implies the main hypothesis *"**H_0A-SR:** Significant differences do not exist in consumers' attitude towards social relationships on social networking sites with respect to their age group"* is not supported.

It can be concluded that there is a significant difference observed in consumers' attitude towards social relationships on social networking sites with respect to their age groups. Different age groups exhibit different attitude and respond in different ways. Interactions with the respondents revealed that youngsters are more attached to weak ties, and avoid their family and relatives on social networks. Moreover youngsters are more interested in making new contacts.

Table 4.33: Summary of Mean Values of All Dimensions of Social Relationships based on Age Group

Years/SR	Social Capital	Tie Strength	Attitude Homophily	Background Homophily	Trust	Normative Influence	Informational Influence
Up to 20	3.20	2.77	2.51	2.58	2.73	2.46	3.00
21-30	3.71	3.15	2.87	2.92	3.02	2.73	3.52
31-40	3.73	3.29	3.01	3.13	3.25	2.65	3.04
More than 40	3.71	2.88	2.68	2.93	3.24	2.34	2.66

As per table 4.40, the mean values are highest in social capital, across all age groups. This results into a conclusion that respondents across all groups show positive response towards social capital factors. The highest mean value (3.73) is acquired by respondents belonging to age group 31-40.

It can be said that social capital may serve as an influential driver across all age groups that affects consumers' use of social networking sites as a vehicle for electronic word of mouth.

4.4.4 Variations in Consumer Attitude towards Electronic Word of Mouth in Social Networks, with respect to Age Group

4.4.4.1 Variations in Consumer Attitude towards Opinion Leading Behavior in Social Networks, with respect to Age Group

The table 4.34 shows the descriptives and the results of 't' test for attitude towards opinion leading behavior in social networks with respect to age group. The mean values, all across the groups are less than 3.00; hence it shows a moderate attitude towards opinion leading behavior.

Table 4.34: Consumer Attitude towards Opinion leading Behavior in Social Networks with respect to Age Group

Age Group	N	Mean	Std. Deviation	F	Sig.	Remark
Up to 20	9	2.11	.902	**7.252**	**.000**	**Significant**
21-30	443	2.65	.835			
31-40	84	2.47	.863			
More than 40	30	2.00	.930			
Total	566	2.58	.859			

The results of ANOVA, as shown above shows that significant difference exists for attitude towards opinion leading behavior in social networks with respect to age group (t=7.252, sig. = .000). Since the associated probability is less than the significance level of 0.05, the null hypothesis *"**H_0A-OL:** Significant differences do not exist in consumers' opinion leading behavior in social networking sites with respect to their age group"* is not supported.

4.4.4.2 Variations in Consumer Attitude towards Opinion Seeking Behavior in Social Networks, with respect to Age Group

The table 4.35 shows the descriptives and the results of 't' test for attitude towards opinion seeking behavior in social networks with respect to age group. The mean values, all across the groups are less than 3.00; hence it shows a moderate attitude towards opinion seeking behavior.

Table 4.35: Consumer Attitude towards Opinion Seeking Behavior in Social Networks with respect to Age Group

Age Group	N	Mean	Std. Deviation	F	Sig.	Remark
Up to 20	9	2.36	.875	10.982	.000	Significant
21-30	443	2.95	.837			
31-40	84	2.72	1.002			
More than 40	30	2.10	.952			
Total	566	2.86	.893			

The results of ANOVA, as shown above shows that significant difference exists for attitude towards opinion seeking behavior in social networks with respect to age group (F=10.982, sig. = .000). Since the associated probability is less than the significance level of 0.05, the null hypothesis *"**H_0A-OS:** Significant differences do not exist in consumers' opinion seeking behavior in social networking sites with respect to their age group"* is not supported.

Overall, the mean of total responses came out to be 2.86, which is on the moderate side of opinion seeking behavior.

4.4.4.3 Variations in Consumer Attitude towards Opinion Passing Behavior in Social Networks, with respect to Age Group

The table 4.36 shows the descriptives and the results of 't' test for attitude towards opinion passing behavior in social networks with respect to age group. The mean values, across the groups: up to 20, 21-30 and 31-40 are more than 3.00; hence it shows somewhat positive attitude towards opinion passing behavior.

Table 4.36: Consumer Attitude towards Opinion Passing Behavior in Social Networks with respect to Age Group

Age Group	N	Mean	Std. Deviation	F	Sig.	Remark
Up to 20	9	3.05	.873	8.735	.000	Significant
21-30	443	3.18	.832			
31-40	84	3.09	.874			
More than 40	30	2.35	1.090			
Total	566	3.12	.872			

The results of ANOVA, as shown above shows that significant difference exists for attitude towards opinion passing behavior in social networks with respect to age group (F=8.735, sig. = .000). Since the associated probability is less than the significance level of

0.05, the null hypothesis *"H_0A-OP: Significant differences do not exist in consumers' opinion passing behavior in social networking sites with respect to their age group"* is not supported.

Overall, the mean of total responses came out to be 3.12, which is somewhat on the positive side of opinion passing behavior.

Table 4.37: Summary of Hypotheses Testing Results based on Consumer Attitude towards Electronic Word of Mouth in Social Networks, with respect to Age Group

	Hypotheses	Result
H_0A-OL	Significant differences do not exist in consumers' opinion leading behavior in social networking sites with respect to their age group.	**Not Supported**
H_0A-OS	Significant differences do not exist in consumers' opinion seeking behavior in social networking sites with respect to their age group.	**Not Supported**
H_0A-OP	Significant differences do not exist in consumers' opinion passing behavior in social networking sites with respect to their age group.	**Not Supported**

Based on the above results, all three sub hypotheses are not supported. This result implies that, the main hypothesis *"H_0A-EWOM: Significant differences do not exist in consumers' electronic word of mouth behavior in social networking sites with respect to their age group"*, is not supported, very strongly. So, there exist strong significant differences among all age groups towards electronic word of mouth behavior in social networking sites.

Social network users who are young are more influenced by their peers, colleagues, friends, etc., whereas people who belong to higher age groups tend to take their own decisions. Rather, elder people take more rational decisions, as compared to younger group.

Young social network users are open to interactions and discussions on social platforms, and are close to weak ties as well. In fact the time spent on social media by different social network users vary, as seen in the results of this research. Electronic word of mouth behavior will be different across different groups.

Table 4.38: Summary of Mean Values of Electronic Word of Mouth Behavior w.r.t Age Group

Age Group/Electronic Word of Mouth	Opinion Leading	Opinion Seeking	Opinion Passing
Up To 20	2.11	2.36	3.05
21-30	2.65	2.95	3.18
31-40	2.47	2.72	3.09
More than 40	2.00	2.10	2.35

As per table 4.38, the mean values amongst opinion leading and opinion seeking are less than 3 in all age groups. The respondents in the age groups: up to 20, 21-30 and 31-40 show somewhat favorable attitude towards electronic word of mouth in social networking sites. The highest mean value (3.18) is acquired by respondents in the age group, 21-30 years, for opinion passing behavior.

Across all the age groups, the mean value of opinion passing behavior was highest amongst opinion leading, opinion seeking and opinion passing behavior. We can infer that consumers are actively involved in content generation on digital platforms. They are ready to pass on the positive and negative reviews on the new media platforms.

4.4.5 Variations in Consumers' Attitude towards Social Relationships on Social Networks with respect to Income

4.4.5.1 Variation in Consumers' Attitude towards Social Capital on Social Networks with respect to Income

The table 4.39 shows the descriptives and ANOVA results for consumers' attitude towards social capital on social networks with respect to income.

The mean values of income amongst groups (Annual income in lakhs): less than 3, 3-6, 6-9, 9-12 and more than 12 exhibit values of 3.69, 3.65, 3.71, 3.81 and 3.77 respectively. This shows that respondents falling in all the income groups have a positive response to social capital.

Table 4.39: Variation in Consumers' Attitude towards Social Capital on Social Networks with respect to Income

Annual Income (In lakhs)	N	Mean	Std. Deviation	F	Sig.	Remark
Less than 3	205	3.69	.599	.803	.523	Not Significant
3-6	139	3.65	.610			
6-9	116	3.71	.570			
9-12	43	3.81	.536			
More than 12	63	3.77	.647			
Total	566	3.70	.597			

ANOVA shows that there is no significant difference in consumers' attitude towards social capital on social networks with respect to income. Since the associated probability is more than the significance level of 0.05 (F= .803, sig. = .523), the null hypothesis *"$H_0$1-SC: Significant differences do not exist in consumers' attitude towards social capital on social networking sites with respect to their income"* is supported.

From a consumer behavior perspective, consumers' reliance on product recommendations and opinions from friends in their personal networks (i.e., reference groups) can be interpreted as evidence of the effect of social capital. Income does not play a significant role in deciding about the same.

The mean values of the respondents across various age groups show positive attitude and behavior towards social capital. The overall mean value is 3.70, which indicates that a positive attitude exists across all income groups.

4.4.5.2 Variation in Consumers' Attitude towards Tie Strength on Social Networks with respect to Income

The table 4.40 shows the descriptives and ANOVA results for consumers' attitude towards tie strength on social networks with respect to income.

The mean values of income amongst groups (Annual income in lakhs): less than 3, 3-6, 6-9, 9-12 and more than 12 exhibit values of 3.18, 3.03, 3.08, 3.38 and 3.33 respectively. This shows that respondents falling in all the income groups have a positive response to tie strength.

Table 4.40: Variation in Consumers' Attitude towards Tie Strength on Social Networks with respect to Income

Annual Income (In lakhs)	N	Mean	Std. Deviation	F	Sig.	Remark
Less than 3	205	3.18	.752	**2.848**	**.023**	**Significant**
3-6	139	3.03	.799			
6-9	116	3.08	.789			
9-12	43	3.38	.738			
More than 12	63	3.33	.889			
Total	566	3.15	.791			

ANOVA shows that there is a significant difference in consumers' attitude towards tie strength on social networks with respect to income. Since the associated probability is less than the significance level of 0.05 (F= 2.848, sig. = .023), the null hypothesis *"H_0I-TS: Significant differences do not exist in consumers' attitude towards tie strength on social networking sites with respect to their income"* is not supported.

The overall mean value is 3.15, which indicates that somewhat positive attitude exists across income groups.

4.4.5.3 Variation in Consumers' Attitude towards Attitude Homophily on Social Networks with respect to Income

The table 4.41 shows the descriptives and ANOVA results for consumers' attitude towards attitude homophily on social networks with respect to income.

The mean values of income amongst groups (Annual income in lakhs): less than 3, 3-6, 6-9, 9-12 and more than 12 exhibit values less than 3. This shows that respondents falling in all the income groups have a moderate response to attitude homophily.

Table 4.41: Variation in Consumers' Attitude towards Attitude Homophily on Social Networks with respect to Income

Annual Income (In lakhs)	N	Mean	Std. Deviation	F	Sig.	Remark
Less than 3	205	2.82	.702	1.047	.382	Not Significant
3-6	139	2.89	.708			
6-9	116	2.94	.679			
9-12	43	2.79	.678			
More than 12	63	2.97	.733			
Total	566	2.88	.701			

ANOVA shows that there is no significant difference in consumers' attitude towards attitude homophily on social networks with respect to income. Since the associated probability is more than the significance level of 0.05 (F= 1.047, sig. = .382), the null hypothesis *"H_0I-AH: Significant differences do not exist in consumers' attitude towards attitude homophily on social networking sites with respect to their income"* is supported. The overall mean value is 2.88, which indicates that somewhat a moderate attitude exists across income groups.

4.4.5.4 Variation in Consumers' Attitude towards Background Homophily on Social Networks with respect to Income

The table 4.42 shows the descriptives and ANOVA results for consumers' attitude towards background homophily on social networks with respect to income.
The mean values of income amongst groups (Annual income in lakhs): less than 3, 3-6, 6-9, 9-12 and more than 12 exhibit values close to 3. This shows that respondents falling in all the income groups have somewhat positive response to attitude homophily.

Table 4.42: Variation in Consumers' attitude towards Background Homophily on Social Networks with respect to Income

Annual Income (In lakhs)	N	Mean	Std. Deviation	F	Sig.	Remark
Less than 3	205	2.90	.666	1.664	.157	Not Significant
3-6	139	2.89	.723			
6-9	116	2.99	.677			
9-12	43	2.97	.763			
More than 12	63	3.13	.741			
Total	566	2.95	.700			

ANOVA shows that there is no significant difference in consumers' attitude towards attitude homophily on social networks with respect to income. Since the associated probability is more than the significance level of 0.05 (F= 1.664, sig. = .157), the null hypothesis *"H_0I-BH: Significant differences do not exist in consumers' attitude towards background homophily on social networking sites with respect to their income"* is supported.

The overall mean value is 2.95, which indicates that somewhat a moderate positive attitude exists across income groups.

4.4.5.5 Variation in Consumers' Attitude towards Trust on Social Networks with respect to Income

The table 4.43 shows the descriptives and ANOVA results for consumers' attitude towards trust on social networks with respect to income.

The mean values of income amongst groups (Annual income in lakhs): less than 3, 3-6, 6-9, 9-12 and more than 12 exhibit values close to 3. This shows that respondents falling in all the income groups have somewhat positive response to trust.

Table 4.43: Variation in Consumers' Attitude towards Trust on Social Networks with respect to Income

Annual Income (In lakhs)	N	Mean	Std. Deviation	F	Sig.	Remark
Less than 3	205	2.97	.751	3.226	.012	Significant
3-6	139	3.05	.763			
6-9	116	3.04	.633			
9-12	43	3.28	.708			
More than 12	63	3.27	.695			
Total	566	3.06	.728			

ANOVA shows that there is a significant difference in consumers' attitude towards trust on social networks with respect to income. Since the associated probability is less than the significance level of 0.05 (F= 3.226, sig. = .012), the null hypothesis *"H_0I-TR: Significant differences do not exist in consumers' attitude towards trust on social networking sites with respect to their income"* is not supported.

The overall mean value is 3.06, which indicates that somewhat a positive attitude exists across income groups.

4.4.5.6 Variation in Consumers' Attitude towards Normative Influence on Social Networks with respect to Income

The table 4.44 shows the descriptives and ANOVA results for consumers' attitude towards normative influence on social networks with respect to income.

The mean values of income amongst groups (Annual income in lakhs): less than 3, 3-6, 6-9, 9-12 and more than 12 exhibit values less than 3. This shows that respondents falling in all the income groups have a moderate response to normative influence.

Table 4.44: Variation in Consumers' Attitude towards Normative Influence on Social Networks with respect to Income

Annual Income (In lakhs)	N	Mean	Std. Deviation	F	Sig.	Remark
Less than 3	205	2.68	.727	**1.883**	**.112**	**Not Significant**
3-6	139	2.62	.869			
6-9	116	2.82	.781			
9-12	43	2.86	.738			
More than 12	63	2.56	1.003			
Total	566	2.70	.812			

ANOVA shows that there is no significant difference in consumers' attitude towards normative influence on social networks with respect to income. Since the associated probability is more than the significance level of 0.05 (F= 1.883, sig. = .112), the null hypothesis *"H_0I-NI: Significant differences do not exist in consumers' attitude towards normative influence on social networking sites with respect to their income"* is supported. The overall mean value is 2.70, which indicates that somewhat a moderate attitude exists across income groups.

4.4.5.7 Variation in Consumers' Attitude towards Informational Influence on Social Networks with respect to Income

The table 4.45 shows the descriptives and ANOVA results for consumers' attitude towards informational influence on social networks with respect to income.

The mean values of income amongst groups (Annual income in lakhs): less than 3, 3-6, 6-9, 9-12 and more than 12 exhibit values between 3.1 and 3.6. This shows that respondents falling in all the income groups have a positive response towards informational influence.

Table 4.45: Variation in Consumers' Attitude towards Informational Influence on Social Networks with respect to Income

Annual Income (In lakhs)	N	Mean	Std. Deviation	F	Sig.	Remark
Less than 3	205	3.58	.820	7.063	.000	Significant
3-6	139	3.18	.987			
6-9	116	3.54	.662			
9-12	43	3.23	.912			
More than 12	63	3.11	1.153			
Total	566	3.39	.904			

ANOVA shows that there is a significant difference in consumers' attitude towards informational influence on social networks with respect to income. Since the associated probability is less than the significance level of 0.05 (F= 7.063, sig. = .000), the null *hypothesis "**H_0I-II:** Significant differences do not exist in consumers' attitude towards informational influence on social networking sites with respect to their income"* is not supported. The overall mean value is 3.39, which indicates that overall a positive attitude exists across income groups.

Table 4.46: Summary of Hypotheses Testing Results based on Consumers' Attitude towards Social Relationships on Social Networks with respect to Income

	Hypotheses	Result
H_0I-SC	Significant differences do not exist in consumers' attitude towards social capital on social networking sites with respect to their income.	Supported
H_0I-TS	Significant differences do not exist in consumers' attitude towards tie strength on social networking sites with respect to their income.	Not Supported
H_0I-AH	Significant differences do not exist in consumers' attitude towards attitude homophily on social networking sites with respect to their income.	Supported
H_0I-BH	Significant differences do not exist in consumers' attitude towards background homophily on social networking sites with respect to their income.	Supported
H_0I-TR	Significant differences do not exist in consumers' attitude towards trust on social networking sites with respect to their income.	Not Supported
H_0I-NI	Significant differences do not exist in consumers' attitude towards normative influence on social networking sites with respect to their income.	Supported

H_0I-II	Significant differences do not exist in consumers' attitude towards informational influence on social networking sites with respect to their income.	**Not Supported**

Based on the above results, four sub hypotheses are supported and three sub hypotheses are not supported. This result implies that, there is a *weak support* towards the main hypothesis *"H_0I-SR: Significant differences do not exist in consumers' attitude towards social relationships on social networking sites with respect to their income".*

So, there is no significant difference observed in consumers' attitude towards social relationships on social networking sites with respect to their income.

Table 4.47: Summary of Mean Values of All Dimensions of Social Relationships based on Income

Annual Income in Lakhs/ SR	Social Capital	Tie Strength	Attitude Homophily	Background Homophily	Trust	Normative Influence	Informational Influence
Less than 3	3.69	3.18	2.82	2.90	2.97	2.68	3.58
3-6	3.65	3.03	2.89	2.89	3.05	2.62	3.18
6-9	3.71	3.08	2.94	2.99	3.04	2.82	3.54
9-12	3.81	3.38	2.79	2.97	3.28	2.86	3.23
More than 12	3.77	3.33	2.97	3.13	3.27	2.56	3.11

As per table 4.47, the mean values are highest in social capital, across all age groups. This results into a conclusion that respondents across all groups based on income show positive response towards social capital factors. The highest mean value (3.81) is acquired by respondents belonging to income group "more than 12", which is towards social capital.

4.4.6 Variations in Consumer Attitude towards Electronic Word of Mouth in Social Networks, with respect to Income

4.4.6.1 Variations in Consumer Attitude towards Opinion Leading Behavior in Social Networks, with respect to Income

The table 4.48 shows the descriptives and the results of 't' test for attitude towards opinion leading behavior in social networks with respect to age group. The mean values, all across the groups are less than 3.00; hence it shows a moderate attitude towards opinion leading behavior.

Table 4.48: Consumer Attitude towards Opinion Leading Behavior in Social Networks with respect to Income

Annual Income (In lakhs)	N	Mean	Std. Deviation	F	Sig.	Remark
Less than 3	205	2.62	.844	.267	.899	Not Significant
3-6	139	2.57	.840			
6-9	116	2.58	.853			
9-12	43	2.55	.773			
More than 12	63	2.50	1.025			
Total	566	2.58	.859			

The results of ANOVA, as shown above shows that significant difference do not exist for attitude towards opinion leading behavior in social networks with respect to income (F=.267, sig. = .899). Since the associated probability is more than the significance level of 0.05, the null hypothesis *"**H_0I-OL:** Significant differences do not exist in consumers' opinion leading behavior in social networking sites with respect to their income"* is supported.

Overall, the mean value is 2.58, which shows that respondents across all income groups have a moderate behavior towards opinion leading behavior.

4.4.6.2 Variations in Consumer Attitude towards Opinion Seeking Behavior in Social Networks, with respect to Income

The table 4.49 shows the descriptives and the results of ANOVA for attitude towards opinion seeking behavior in social networks with respect to age group. The mean values, all across the groups are less than 3.00; hence it shows a moderate attitude towards opinion seeking behavior.

Table 4.49: Consumer Attitude towards Opinion Seeking Behavior in Social Networks with respect to Income

Annual Income (In lakhs)	N	Mean	Std. Deviation	F	Sig.	Remark
Less than 3	205	2.93	.841	**1.335**	**.256**	**Not Significant**
3-6	139	2.79	.918			
6-9	116	2.95	.873			
9-12	43	2.76	.828			
More than 12	63	2.73	1.056			
Total	566	2.86	.893			

The results of ANOVA, as shown above shows that significant difference does not exist for attitude towards opinion seeking behavior in social networks with respect to age group (F=1.335, sig. = .256). Since the associated probability is more than the significance level of 0.05, the null hypothesis *"H_0I-OS: Significant differences do not exist in consumers' opinion seeking behavior in social networking sites with respect to their income"* is supported.

Overall, the mean of total responses came out to be 2.86, which is on the moderate side of opinion seeking behavior.

4.4.6.3 Variations in Consumer Attitude towards Opinion Passing Behavior in Social Networks, with respect to Income

The table 4.50 shows the descriptives and the results of 'ANOVA for attitude towards opinion passing behavior in social networks with respect to age group. The mean values, across the groups are between 2.9 and 3.2; hence it shows somewhat positive attitude and behavior towards opinion passing behavior.

Table 4.50: Consumer Attitude towards Opinion Passing Behavior in Social Networks with respect to Income

Annual Income (In lakhs)	N	Mean	Std. Deviation	F	Sig.	Remark
Less than 3	205	3.19	.836	**1.622**	**.167**	**Not Significant**
3-6	139	3.12	.879			
6-9	116	3.15	.861			
9-12	43	3.00	.839			
More than 12	63	2.90	.986			
Total	566	3.12	.872			

The results of ANOVA, as shown above shows that significant difference do not exist for attitude and behavior towards opinion passing behavior in social networks with respect to income (F=1.622, sig. = .167). Since the associated probability is more than the significance level of 0.05, the null hypothesis *"**H_0I-OP:** Significant differences do not exist in consumers' opinion passing behavior in social networking sites with respect to their income"* is supported.

Overall, the mean of total responses came out to be 3.12, which is somewhat on the positive side of opinion passing behavior.

Table 4.51: Summary of Hypotheses Testing Results based on Consumer Attitude towards Electronic Word of Mouth in Social Networks, with respect to Income

	Hypotheses	Result
H_0I-OL	Significant differences do not exist in consumers' opinion leading behavior in social networking sites with respect to their income.	**Supported**
H_0I-OS	Significant differences do not exist in consumers' opinion seeking behavior in social networking sites with respect to their income.	**Supported**
H_0I-OP	Significant differences do not exist in consumers' opinion passing behavior in social networking sites with respect to their income.	**Supported**

Based on the above results, all three sub hypotheses are supported. This result implies that, the main hypothesis *"**H_0I-EWOM:** Significant differences do not exist in consumers' electronic word of mouth behavior in social networking sites with respect to their income"*, is supported, very strongly.

Electronic word of mouth behavior (opinion leading, opinion seeking and opinion passing behavior) amongst social network users are not affected by the income.

Most of the respondents belong to younger age group (less than 35) and a good number of young respondents were students. The results reveal that overall, income plays an insignificant role.

Marketers need to devise strategies on social media considering the fact that income will not impact the online behavior (providing and seeking opinion) of social network users.

Table 4.52: Summary of Mean Values of Electronic Word of Mouth Behavior with respect to Income

Annual Income in Lakhs/Electronic Word of Mouth	Opinion Leading	Opinion Seeking	Opinion Passing
Less than 3	2.62	2.93	3.19
3-6	2.57	2.79	3.12
6-9	2.58	2.95	3.15
9-12	2.55	2.76	3.00
More than 12	2.50	2.73	2.90

As per table 4.52, the mean values amongst opinion leading and opinion seeking are less than 3 in all age groups. The respondents in in all the age groups show somewhat favorable attitude and behavior towards opinion passing behavior in social networking sites. The highest mean value (3.19) is acquired by respondents in the income group, less than 3, for opinion passing behavior.

Means of opinion passing behavior in all income groups are highest among opinion giving, opinion seeking and opinion passing behavior.

4.4.7 Variations in Consumers' Attitude towards Social Relationships on Social Networks with respect to Education

Those who have higher levels of education are more likely to be employed full-time and may be more concerned with the intersection of personal and professional contacts and content on social media. Previous research from Pew Internet has shown that those with the highest education levels are also more likely to have a job that specifically requires them to self-promote or market themselves online. These "public personae" may be especially cautious about avoiding any privacy missteps on social media.

4.4.7.1 Variation in Consumers' Attitude towards Social Capital on Social Networks with respect to Education

The table 4.53 shows the descriptives and ANOVA results for consumers' attitude towards social capital on social networks with respect to education.

The mean value of highest education amongst all the groups is more than 3 (between 3.1 and 3.8). This shows that respondents falling in various education groups have a positive response to social capital.

Table 4.53: Variation in Consumers' Attitude towards Social Capital on Social Networks with respect to Education

Highest Education	N	Mean	Std. Deviation	F	Sig.	Remark
High School	4	3.10	.759	1.766	.134	Not Significant
Graduate	143	3.73	.584			
Post Graduate	382	3.71	.585			
Higher Studies	34	3.54	.722			
Any Other	3	3.76	.577			
Total	566	3.70	.597			

ANOVA shows that there is no significant difference in consumers' attitude towards social capital on social networks with respect to education. Since the associated probability is more than the significance level of 0.05 (F= 1.766, sig. = .134), the null hypothesis "***H_0E-SC:*** *Significant differences do not exist in consumers' attitude towards social capital on social networking sites with respect to their education*" is supported.

The mean values of the respondents across various age groups show positive attitude and behavior towards social capital. The overall mean value is 3.70, which indicates that a positive attitude towards social capital exists across all educational groups.

4.4.7.2 Variation in Consumers' Attitude towards Tie Strength on Social Networks with respect to Education

The table 4.54 shows the descriptives and ANOVA results for consumers' attitude towards tie strength on social networks with respect to education.

The mean values of education amongst groups (highest education): graduate, post graduate, higher studies exhibit values of 3.21, 3.16, 3.08 and 3.07 respectively. This shows that respondents falling in these education groups have a positive response to tie strength.

Table 4.54: Variation in Consumers' Attitude towards Tie Strength on Social Networks with respect to Education

Highest Education	N	Mean	Std. Deviation	F	Sig.	Remark
High School	4	2.13	1.031	**2.244**	**.063**	**Not Significant**
Graduate	143	3.21	.735			
Post Graduate	382	3.16	.796			
Higher Studies	34	3.07	.854			
Any Other	3	2.67	1.258			
Total	566	3.16	.792			

ANOVA shows that there is no significant difference in consumers' attitude towards tie strength on social networks with respect to education. Since the associated probability is more than the significance level of 0.05 (F= 2.244, sig. = .063), the null hypothesis *"**H_0E-TS:** Significant differences do not exist in consumers' attitude towards tie strength on social networking sites with respect to their education"* is supported.

The overall mean value is 3.16, which indicates that somewhat positive attitude exists across education groups.

4.4.7.3 Variation in Consumers' Attitude towards Attitude Homophily on Social Networks with respect to Education

The table 4.55 shows the descriptives and ANOVA results for consumers' attitude towards attitude homophily on social networks with respect to education.

The mean values of education amongst all the groups are less than 3, but more than 2.5. This shows that respondents falling in all the groups have a moderate response to attitude homophily.

Table 4.55: Variation in Consumers' Attitude towards Attitude Homophily on Social Networks with respect to Education

Highest Education	N	Mean	Std. Deviation	F	Sig.	Remark
High School	4	2.50	1.139	.897	.466	Not Significant
Graduate	143	2.83	.721			
Post Graduate	382	2.92	.700			
Higher Studies	34	2.79	.580			
Any Other	3	2.78	.694			
Total	566	2.88	.701			

ANOVA shows that there is no significant difference in consumers' attitude towards attitude homophily on social networks with respect to education. Since the associated probability is more than the significance level of 0.05 (F= .897, sig. = .466), the null hypothesis *"H_0E-AH: Significant differences do not exist in consumers' attitude towards attitude homophily on social networking sites with respect to their education"* is supported. The overall mean value is 2.88, which indicates that somewhat a moderate attitude exists across all education groups.

4.4.7.4 Variation in Consumers' Attitude towards Background Homophily on Social Networks with respect to Education

The table 4.56 shows the descriptives and ANOVA results for consumers' attitude towards background homophily on social networks with respect to education.

The mean values of education amongst all groups are close to 3. This shows that respondents falling in all the education groups have somewhat positive response to attitude homophily.

Table 4.56: Variation in Consumers' Attitude towards Background Homophily on Social Networks with respect to Education

Highest Education	N	Mean	Std. Deviation	F	Sig.	Remark
High School	4	2.25	1.041	1.196	.312	Not Significant
Graduate	143	2.97	.712			
Post Graduate	382	2.95	.702			
Higher Studies	34	3.03	.560			
Any Other	3	2.75	.901			
Total	566	2.95	.701			

ANOVA shows that there is no significant difference in consumers' attitude towards background homophily on social networks with respect to education. Since the associated probability is more than the significance level of 0.05 (F= 1.196, sig. = .312), the null hypothesis *"H_0I-BH: Significant differences do not exist in consumers' attitude towards background homophily on social networking sites with respect to their education"* is supported.

The overall mean value is 2.95, which indicates that somewhat a positive attitude exists across education groups.

4.4.7.5 Variation in Consumers' Attitude towards Trust on Social Networks with respect to Education

The table 4.57 shows the descriptives and ANOVA results for consumers' attitude towards trust on social networks with respect to education.

The mean values of education amongst groups: high school, graduates, post graduates, higher studies, is close to 3. This shows that respondents falling in all the education groups have somewhat positive response to trust.

Table 4.57: Variation in Consumers' Attitude towards Trust on Social Networks with respect to Education

Highest Education	N	Mean	Std. Deviation	F	Sig.	Remark
High School	4	2.20	.282	1.505	.199	Not Significant
Graduate	143	3.04	.793			
Post Graduate	382	3.08	.696			
Higher Studies	34	3.05	.762			
Any Other	3	3.00	1.200			
Total	566	3.06	.728			

ANOVA shows that there is no significant difference in consumers' attitude towards trust on social networks with respect to education. Since the associated probability is more than the significance level of 0.05 (F= 1.505, sig. = .199), the null hypothesis *"H_0E-TR: Significant differences do not exist in consumers' attitude towards trust on social networking sites with respect to their education"* is supported.

The overall mean value is 3.06, which indicates that somewhat a positive attitude exists across education groups.

4.4.7.6 Variation in Consumers' Attitude towards Normative Influence on Social Networks with respect to Education

The table 4.58 shows the descriptives and ANOVA results for consumers' attitude towards normative influence on social networks with respect to education.

The mean values of all the groups are less than 3. This shows that respondents falling in all the education groups, except high school (M=1.96) and others (M=1.9) have a moderate response to normative influence.

Table 4.58: Variation in Consumers' attitude towards Normative Influence on Social Networks with respect to Education

Highest Education	N	Mean	Std. Deviation	F	Sig.	Remark
High School	4	1.96	.759	4.212	.002	Significant
Graduate	143	2.71	.779			
Post Graduate	382	2.74	.809			
Higher Studies	34	2.28	.835			
Any Other	3	1.90	.719			
Total	566	2.70	.812			

ANOVA shows that there is a significant difference in consumers' attitude towards normative influence on social networks with respect to education. Since the associated probability is less than the significance level of 0.05 (F= 4.212, sig. = .002), the null hypothesis *"H_0E-NI: Significant differences do not exist in consumers' attitude towards normative influence on social networking sites with respect to their education"* is not supported.

The overall mean value is 2.70, which indicates that somewhat a moderate attitude towards normative influence exists across all education groups.

4.4.7.7 Variation in Consumers' attitude towards Informational Influence on Social Networks with respect to Education

The table 4.59 shows the descriptives and ANOVA results for consumers' attitude towards informational influence on social networks with respect to education.

The mean values in the groups: graduate and post graduates are 3.56 and 3.39 respectively. This shows that respondents falling in these two groups have a positive response towards informational influence.

Table 4.59: Variation in Consumers' attitude towards Informational Influence on Social Networks with respect to Education

Highest Education	N	Mean	Std. Deviation	F	Sig.	Remark
High School	4	2.66	1.247	**5.219**	**.000**	**Significant**
Graduate	143	3.56	.846			
Post Graduate	382	3.39	.886			
Higher Studies	34	2.97	1.095			
Any Other	3	2.22	.384			
Total	566	3.39	.904			

ANOVA shows that there is a significant difference in consumers' attitude towards informational influence on social networks with respect to education. Since the associated probability is less than the significance level of 0.05 (F= 5.219, sig. = .000), the null hypothesis *"**H_0E-II:** Significant differences do not exist in consumers' attitude towards informational influence on social networking sites with respect to their education"* is not supported. The overall mean value is 3.39, which indicates that overall a positive attitude exists across education groups.

Table 4.60: Summary of Hypotheses Testing Results based on Consumers' Attitude towards Social Relationships on Social Networks with respect to Education

	Hypotheses	Result
H_0E-SC	Significant differences do not exist in consumers' attitude towards social capital on social networking sites with respect to their education.	**Supported**
H_0E-TS	Significant differences do not exist in consumers' attitude towards tie strength on social networking sites with respect to their education.	**Supported**
H_0E-AH	Significant differences do not exist in consumers' attitude towards attitude homophily on social networking sites with respect to their education.	**Supported**

H_0E-BH	Significant differences do not exist in consumers' attitude towards background homophily on social networking sites with respect to their education.	**Supported**
H_0E-TR	Significant differences do not exist in consumers' attitude towards trust on social networking sites with respect to their education.	**Supported**
H_0E-NI	Significant differences do not exist in consumers' attitude towards normative influence on social networking sites with respect to their education.	**Not Supported**
H_0E-II	Significant differences do not exist in consumers' attitude towards informational influence on social networking sites with respect to their education.	**Not Supported**

Based on the above results, five sub hypotheses are supported and two sub hypotheses are not supported. This result implies that, there exists a moderate support towards the main hypothesis *"**H_0E-SR:** Significant differences do not exist in consumers' attitude towards social relationships on social networking sites with respect to their education".*

So, there is no significant difference observed in consumers' attitude towards social relationships on social networking sites with respect to their education. Education was found to be insignificant towards consumer receptivity to social relationship variables.

Table 4.61: Summary of Mean Values of All Dimensions of Social Relationships based on Education

Highest Education/ SR	**Social Capital**	**Tie Strength**	**Attitude Homophily**	**Background Homophily**	**Trust**	**Normative Influence**	**Informational Influence**
High School	3.10	2.13	2.50	2.25	2.20	1.96	2.66
Graduate	3.73	3.21	2.83	2.97	3.04	2.71	3.56
Post Graduate	3.71	3.16	2.92	2.95	3.08	2.74	3.39
Higher Studies	3.54	3.07	2.79	3.03	3.05	2.28	2.97
Any Other	3.76	2.67	2.78	2.75	3.00	1.90	2.22

As per table 4.61, the mean values are highest in social capital, across all age groups. This results into a conclusion that respondents across all groups based on education show positive response towards social capital factors. The highest mean value (3.76) is for social capital, which is exhibited by respondents belonging to "others" category.

4.4.8 Variations in Consumer Attitude towards Electronic Word of Mouth in Social Networks, with respect to Education

4.4.8.1 Variations in Consumer Attitude towards Opinion Leading Behavior in Social Networks, with respect to Education

The table 4.62 shows the descriptives and the results of ANOVA for attitude towards opinion leading behavior in social networks with respect to education. The mean values, all across the groups are less than 3.00; hence it shows a moderate attitude towards opinion leading behavior.

Table 4.62: Consumer Attitude towards Opinion Leading Behavior in Social Networks with respect to Education

Highest Education	N	Mean	Std. Deviation	F	Sig.	Remark
High School	4	1.50	.842	**5.608**	**.000**	**Significant**
Graduate	143	2.56	.873			
Post Graduate	382	2.66	.843			
Higher Studies	34	2.07	.768			
Any Other	3	2.17	.722			
Total	566	2.59	.860			

The results of ANOVA, as shown above shows that a significant difference exists for attitude towards opinion leading behavior in social networks with respect to education (F= 5.608, sig. = .000). Since the associated probability is less than the significance level of 0.05, the null hypothesis *"**H_0E-OL:** Significant differences do not exist in consumers' opinion leading behavior in social networking sites with respect to their education"* is not supported.

Overall, the mean value is 2.59, which shows that respondents across all education groups have a moderate behavior towards opinion leading behavior.

4.4.8.2 Variations in Consumer Attitude towards Opinion Seeking Behavior in Social Networks, with respect to Education

The table 4.63 shows the descriptives and the results of ANOVA test for attitude towards opinion seeking behavior in social networks with respect to age group. The mean values, all across the groups are less than 3.00; hence it shows a moderate attitude and behavior towards opinion seeking behavior.

Table 4.63: Consumer Attitude towards Opinion Seeking Behavior in Social Networks with respect to Education

Highest Education	N	Mean	Std. Deviation	F	Sig.	Remark
High School	4	2.00	1.224	3.664	.006	Significant
Graduate	143	2.96	.855			
Post Graduate	382	2.88	.901			
Higher Studies	34	2.47	.789			
Any Other	3	2.08	.629			
Total	566	2.86	.893			

The results of ANOVA, as shown above shows that significant difference does not exist for attitude and behavior towards opinion seeking behavior in social networks with respect to education (F=3.664, sig. = .006). Since the associated probability is less than the significance level of 0.05, the null hypothesis *"**H_0E-OS:** Significant differences do not exist in consumers' opinion seeking behavior in social networking sites with respect to their education"* is not supported.

Overall, the mean of total responses came out to be 2.86, which is on the moderate side of opinion seeking behavior.

4.4.8.3 Variations in Consumer Attitude towards Opinion Passing Behavior in Social Networks, with respect to Education

The table 4.64 shows the descriptives and the results of ANOVA test for attitude towards opinion passing behavior in social networks with respect to education. The mean values, of the groups: graduates and post graduates are 3.11 and 3.17 respectively; hence it shows somewhat positive attitude towards opinion passing behavior.

Table 4.64: Consumer Attitude towards Opinion Passing Behavior in Social Networks with respect to Education

Highest Education	N	Mean	Std. Deviation	F	Sig.	Remark
High School	4	2.50	1.080	3.615	.006	Significant
Graduate	143	3.11	.843			
Post Graduate	382	3.17	.852			
Higher Studies	34	2.66	1.012			
Any Other	3	2.50	1.322			
Total	566	3.12	.872			

The results of ANOVA, as shown above shows that significant difference does not exist for attitude towards opinion seeking behavior in social networks with respect to education (F=3.615, sig. = .006). Since the associated probability is less than the significance level of 0.05, the null hypothesis *"**H_0E-OP:** Significant differences do not exist in consumers' opinion passing behavior in social networking sites with respect to their education"* is not supported.

Overall, the mean of total responses came out to be 3.12, which is somewhat on the positive side of opinion passing behavior.

Table 4.65: Summary of Hypotheses Testing Results based on Consumer Attitude towards Electronic Word of Mouth in Social Networks, with respect to Education

	Hypotheses	**Result**
H_0E-OL	Significant differences do not exist in consumers' opinion leading behavior in social networking sites with respect to their education.	**Not Supported**
H_0E-OS	Significant differences do not exist in consumers' opinion seeking behavior in social networking sites with respect to their education.	**Not Supported**
H_0E-OP	Significant differences do not exist in consumers' opinion passing behavior in social networking sites with respect to their education.	**Not Supported**

Based on the above results, all three sub hypotheses are not supported. This result implies that, the main hypothesis *"**H_0E-EWOM:** Significant differences do not exist in consumers' electronic word of mouth behavior in social networking sites with respect to their education"*, is not supported, very strongly.

So, there exists a strong significant difference in consumers' electronic word of mouth behavior in social networking sites with respect to their education. As mentioned in the beginning of this section, people who are more educated are more informed, and they tend to participate more in content generation on social networks.

Table 4.66: Summary of Mean Values of Electronic Word of Mouth Behavior w.r.t Education

Highest Education/SR	Opinion Leading	Opinion Seeking	Opinion Passing
High School	1.50	2.00	2.50
Graduate	2.56	2.96	3.11
Post Graduate	2.66	2.88	3.17
Higher Studies	2.07	2.47	2.66
Any Other	2.17	2.08	2.50

As per table 4.66, the mean values amongst opinion leading and opinion seeking are less than 3 in all age groups. The respondents in in all the age groups show somewhat favorable attitude and behavior towards opinion passing behavior in social networking sites. The highest mean value (3.17) is acquired by respondents in the group, "Post Graduate", for opinion passing behavior.

The mean values of opinion passing behavior were highest amongst all education groups.

4.4.9 Variations in Consumers' Attitude towards Social Relationships on Social Networks with respect to Occupation

4.4.9.1 Variation in Consumers' Attitude towards Social Capital on Social Networks with respect to Occupation

The table 4.67 shows the descriptives and ANOVA results for consumers' attitude towards social capital on social networks with respect to occupation.

Occupation groups: students (M=3.69), service (M= 3.73), self-employed (M=3.69), and retired/not working (M= .02), somewhat exhibit positive response to social capital.

Table 4.67: Variation in Consumers' Attitude towards Social Capital on Social Networks with respect to Occupation

Occupation	N	Mean	Std. Deviation	F	Sig.	Remark
Student	239	3.69	.577	2.322	.056	Not Significant
Service	304	3.73	.604			
Self Employed	17	3.69	.534			
Home Maker	1	2.85	.			
Retired/Not Working/Others	5	3.02	.938			
Total	566	3.70	.597			

ANOVA shows that there is no significant difference in consumers' attitude towards social capital on social networks with respect to occupation. Since the associated probability is more than the significance level of 0.05 (F= 2.322, sig. = .056), the null hypothesis *"**H_0O-SC:** Significant differences do not exist in consumers' attitude towards social capital on social networking sites with respect to their occupation"* is supported.

The overall mean value is 3.70, which indicates that a positive attitude towards social capital exists across all occupational groups.

4.4.9.2 Variation in Consumers' Attitude towards Tie Strength on Social Networks with respect to Occupation

The table 4.68 shows the descriptives and ANOVA results for consumers' attitude towards tie strength on social networks with respect to occupation.

The mean values of occupational groups: student, service, self-employed, home maker exhibit values of 3.14, 3.19, 3.15 and 3.00 respectively. This shows that respondents falling in these occupational groups have a positive response to tie strength.

Table 4.68: Variation in Consumers' attitude towards Tie Strength on Social Networks with respect to Occupation

Occupation	N	Mean	Std. Deviation	F	Sig.	Remark
Student	239	3.14	.729	**2.920**	**.021**	**Significant**
Service	304	3.19	.833			
Self Employed	17	3.15	.745			
Home Maker	1	3.00	.			
Retired/Not Working/Others	5	2.00	.612			
Total	566	3.16	.792			

ANOVA shows that there is a significant difference in consumers' attitude towards tie strength on social networks with respect to occupation. Since the associated probability is less than the significance level of 0.05 (F= 2.920, sig. = .021), the null hypothesis *"H_0O-TS: Significant differences do not exist in consumers' attitude towards tie strength on social networking sites with respect to their occupation"* is not supported.

The overall mean value is 3.16, which indicates that somewhat positive attitude exists across occupation groups.

4.4.9.3 Variation in Consumers' Attitude towards Attitude Homophily on Social Networks with respect to Occupation

The table 4.69 shows the descriptives and ANOVA results for consumers' attitude towards attitude homophily on social networks with respect to education.

The mean values of occupation amongst all the groups are less than 3, but more than 2.5. This shows that respondents falling in all the groups have a moderate response to attitude homophily.

Table 4.69: Variation in Consumers' Attitude towards Attitude Homophily on Social Networks with respect to Occupation

Occupation	N	Mean	Std. Deviation	F	Sig.	Remark
Student	239	2.87	.696	**.220**	**.927**	**Not Significant**
Service	304	2.90	.702			
Self Employed	17	2.76	.797			
Home Maker	1	2.67	.			
Retired/Not Working/Others	5	2.80	.837			
Total	566	2.88	.701			

ANOVA shows that there is no significant difference in consumers' attitude towards attitude homophily on social networks with respect to occupation. Since the associated probability is more than the significance level of 0.05 (F= .220, sig. = .927), the null hypothesis *"H_0O-AH: Significant differences do not exist in consumers' attitude towards attitude homophily on social networking sites with respect to their occupation"* is supported.

The overall mean value is 2.88, which indicates that somewhat a moderate attitude exists across all occupation groups.

4.4.9.4 Variation in Consumers' Attitude towards Background Homophily on Social Networks with respect to Occupation

The table 4.70 shows the descriptives and ANOVA results for consumers' attitude towards background homophily on social networks with respect to occupation.

The mean values of education amongst all groups are close to 3. This shows that respondents falling in all the occupation groups have somewhat positive response to attitude homophily.

Table 4.70: Variation in Consumers' Attitude towards Background Homophily on Social Networks with respect to Occupation

Occupation	N	Mean	Std. Deviation	F	Sig.	Remark
Student	239	2.94	.689	2.393	.050	Significant
Service	304	2.99	.699			
Self Employed	17	2.50	.805			
Home Maker	1	3.25	.			
Retired/Not Working/Others	5	2.60	.548			
Total	566	2.95	.701			

ANOVA shows that there is a significant difference in consumers' attitude towards background homophily on social networks with respect to occupation. Since the associated probability is equal to the significance level of 0.05 (F= 2.393, sig. = .050), the null hypothesis *"H_0O-BH: Significant differences do not exist in consumers' attitude towards background homophily on social networking sites with respect to their occupation"* is not supported.

The overall mean value is 2.95, which indicates that somewhat a positive attitude exists across occupation groups.

4.4.9.5 Variation in Consumers' Attitude towards Trust on Social Networks with respect to Occupation

The table 4.71 shows the descriptives and ANOVA results for consumers' attitude towards trust on social networks with respect to occupation.

The mean values of occupational groups: service, self-employed, home maker exhibit values of 3.13, 3.27, 3.00 respectively. This shows that respondents falling in these groups have somewhat positive response towards trust.

Table 4.71: Variation in Consumers' Attitude towards Trust on Social Networks with respect to Occupation

Occupation	N	Mean	Std. Deviation	F	Sig.	Remark
Student	239	2.97	.746	**3.419**	**.009**	**Significant**
Service	304	3.13	.709			
Self Employed	17	3.27	.670			
Home Maker	1	3.00	.			
Retired/Not Working/Others	5	2.28	.303			
Total	566	3.06	.728			

ANOVA shows that there is a significant difference in consumers' attitude towards trust on social networks with respect to occupation. Since the associated probability is less than the significance level of 0.05 (F= 3.419, sig. = .009), the null hypothesis *"H_0O-TR: Significant differences do not exist in consumers' attitude towards trust on social networking sites with respect to their occupation"* is not supported.

The overall mean value is 3.06, which indicates that somewhat a positive attitude exists across occupation groups.

4.4.9.6 Variation in Consumers' Attitude towards Normative Influence on Social Networks with respect to Occupation

The table 4.72 shows the descriptives and ANOVA results for consumers' attitude towards normative influence on social networks with respect to occupation.

The mean values of all the groups are less than 3. This shows that respondents falling in all the occupation groups have a moderate response to normative influence.

Table 4.72: Variation in Consumers' Attitude towards Normative Influence on Social Networks with respect to Occupation

Occupation	N	Mean	Std. Deviation	F	Sig.	Remark
Student	239	2.72	.737	.439	.781	Not Significant
Service	304	2.69	.865			
Self Employed	17	2.68	.791			
Home Maker	1	2.28	.			
Retired/Not Working/Others	5	2.28	1.115			
Total	566	2.70	.812			

ANOVA shows that there is no significant difference in consumers' attitude towards normative influence on social networks with respect to occupation. Since the associated probability is more than the significance level of 0.05 (F= .439, sig. = .781), the null hypothesis *"H_0O-NI: Significant differences do not exist in consumers' attitude towards normative influence on social networking sites with respect to their occupation"* is supported.

The overall mean value is 2.70, which indicates that somewhat a moderate attitude exists across all occupation groups.

4.4.9.7 Variation in Consumers' Attitude towards Informational Influence on Social Networks with respect to Occupation

The table 4.73 shows the descriptives and ANOVA results for consumers' attitude towards informational influence on social networks with respect to Occupation. The mean values in the groups: student, service, self-employed, home maker are more than 3. This shows that respondents falling in these groups have a positive response towards informational influence.

Table 4.73: Variation in Consumers' Attitude towards Informational Influence on Social Networks with respect to Occupation

Occupation	N	Mean	Std. Deviation	F	Sig.	Remark
Student	239	3.57	.780	4.978	.001	Significant
Service	304	3.29	.959			
Self Employed	17	3.07	.909			
Home Maker	1	3.66	.			
Retired/Not Working/Others	5	2.60	1.516			
Total	566	3.39	.904			

ANOVA shows that there is a significant difference in consumers' attitude towards informational influence on social networks with respect to occupation. Since the associated probability is less than the significance level of 0.05 (F= 4.978, sig. = .001), the null hypothesis *"**H_0O-II:** Significant differences do not exist in consumers' attitude towards informational influence on social networking sites with respect to their occupation"* is not supported.

The overall mean value is 3.39, which indicates that overall a positive attitude exists across occupation groups.

Table 4.74: Summary of Hypotheses Testing Results based on Consumers' Attitude towards Social Relationships on Social Networks with respect to Occupation

	Hypotheses	**Result**
H_0O-SC	Significant differences do not exist in consumers' attitude towards social capital on social networking sites with respect to their occupation.	**Supported**
H_0O-TS	Significant differences do not exist in consumers' attitude towards tie strength on social networking sites with respect to their occupation.	**Not Supported**
H_0O-AH	Significant differences do not exist in consumers' attitude towards attitude homophily on social networking sites with respect to their occupation.	**Supported**
H_0O-BH	Significant differences do not exist in consumers' attitude towards background homophily on social networking sites with respect to their occupation.	**Not Supported**
H_0O-TR	Significant differences do not exist in consumers' attitude towards trust on social networking sites with respect to their occupation.	**Not Supported**
H_0O-NI	Significant differences do not exist in consumers' attitude towards normative influence on social networking sites with respect to their occupation.	**Supported**
H_0O-II	Significant differences do not exist in consumers' attitude towards informational influence on social networking sites with respect to their occupation.	**Not Supported**

Based on the above results, three sub hypotheses are supported and four sub hypotheses are not supported. This result implies that, the main hypothesis

"H_0O-SR: Significant differences do not exist in consumers' attitude towards social relationships on social networking sites with respect to their occupation", is not supported. So, there is a significant difference observed in consumers' attitude towards social relationships on social networking sites with respect to their occupation.

Occupation is a significant demographic variable, as many times occupation and education are interrelated. People tend to manage good relationships on social networks, and it even becomes more important, when people are either in corporate jobs, or doing professional courses.

Table 4.75: Summary of Mean Values of All Dimensions of Social Relationships based on Occupation

Occupation/SR	Social Capital	Tie Strength	Attitude Homophily	Back ground Homophily	Trust	Normative Influence	Informati onal Influence
Student	3.69	3.14	2.87	2.94	2.97	2.72	3.57
Service	3.73	3.19	2.90	2.99	3.13	2.69	3.29
Self Employed	3.69	3.15	2.76	2.50	3.27	2.68	3.07
Home Maker	2.85	3.00	2.67	3.25	3.00	2.28	3.66
Retired/Not Working/ Others	3.02	2.00	2.80	2.60	2.28	2.28	2.60

As per table 4.75, the mean values are highest in social capital, across all age groups except home makers. This results into a conclusion that respondents across all groups based on occupation show positive response towards social capital factors. The highest mean value (3.73) is for social capital, which is exhibited by respondents belonging to "Service" category.

4.4.10 Variations in Consumer Attitude towards Electronic Word of Mouth in Social Networks, with respect to Occupation

4.4.10.1 Variations in Consumer Attitude towards Opinion Leading Behavior in Social Networks, with respect to Occupation

The table 4.76 shows the descriptives and the results of ANOVA for attitude towards opinion leading behavior in social networks with respect to occupation. The mean values, all across the groups are less than 3.00; hence they show a moderate attitude towards opinion leading behavior.

Table 4.76: Consumer Attitude towards Opinion Leading Behavior in Social Networks with respect to Occupation

Occupation	N	Mean	Std. Deviation	F	Sig.	Remark
Student	239	2.65	.837	**1.213**	**.304**	**Not Significant**
Service	304	2.54	.865			
Self Employed	17	2.72	1.000			
Home Maker	1	2.00	.			
Retired/Not Working/Others	5	2.05	1.067			
Total	566	2.59	.860			

The results of ANOVA, as shown above shows that a significant difference exists for attitude towards opinion leading behavior in social networks with respect to occupation (F= 1.213, sig. = .304). Since the associated probability is more than the significance level of 0.05, the null hypothesis *"**H_0O-OL:** Significant differences do not exist in consumers' opinion leading behavior in social networking sites with respect to their occupation"* is supported.

Overall, the mean value is 2.59, which shows that respondents across all occupation groups have a moderate attitude towards opinion leading behavior.

4.4.10.2 Variations in Consumer Attitude towards Opinion Seeking Behavior in Social Networks, with respect to Occupation

The table 4.77 shows the descriptives and the results of ANOVA test for attitude towards opinion seeking behavior in social networks with respect to age group. The mean values, all across the groups are less than 3.00; hence it shows a moderate attitude towards opinion seeking behavior.

Table 4.77: Consumer Attitude towards Opinion Seeking Behavior in Social Networks with respect to Occupation

Occupation	N	Mean	Std. Deviation	F	Sig.	Remark
Student	239	2.96	.825	2.519	.040	Significant
Service	304	2.82	.921			
Self Employed	17	2.76	1.112			
Home Maker	1	2.00	.			
Retired/Not Working/Others	5	1.95	.908			
Total	566	2.86	.893			

The results of ANOVA, as shown above shows that a significant difference exists for attitude towards opinion seeking behavior in social networks with respect to occupation (F=2.519, sig. = .040). Since the associated probability is less than the significance level of 0.05, the null hypothesis *"H_0O-OS: Significant differences do not exist in consumers' opinion seeking behavior in social networking sites with respect to their occupation"* is not supported.

Overall, the mean of total responses came out to be 2.86, which is on the moderate side of opinion seeking behavior.

4.4.10.3 Variations in Consumer Attitude towards Opinion Passing Behavior in Social Networks, with respect to Occupation

The table 4.78 shows the descriptives and the results of ANOVA test for attitude towards opinion passing behavior in social networks with respect to occupation. The mean values, of the groups: student, service, self-employed are 3.21, 3.06 and 3.11 respectively; hence these groups show somewhat positive attitude towards opinion passing behavior.

Table 4.78: Consumer Attitude towards Opinion Passing Behavior in Social Networks with respect to Occupation

Occupation	N	Mean	Std. Deviation	F	Sig.	Remark
Student	239	3.21	.794	1.969	.098	Not Significant
Service	304	3.06	.920			
Self Employed	17	3.11	.940			
Home Maker	1	2.50	.			
Retired/Not Working/Others	5	2.40	.821			
Total	566	3.12	.872			

The results of ANOVA, as shown above shows that significant difference does not exist for attitude towards opinion passing behavior in social networks with respect to occupation (F=1.969, sig. = .098). Since the associated probability is more than the significance level of 0.05, the null hypothesis *"**H_0O-OP:** Significant differences do not exist in consumers' opinion passing behavior in social networking sites with respect to their occupation"* is supported.

Overall, the mean of total responses came out to be 3.12, which is somewhat on the positive side of opinion passing behavior.

Table 4.79: Summary of Hypotheses Testing Results based on Consumer Attitude towards Electronic Word of Mouth in Social Networks, with respect to Occupation

	Hypotheses	**Result**
H_0O-OL	Significant differences do not exist in consumers' opinion leading behavior in social networking sites with respect to their occupation.	**Supported**
H_0O-OS	Significant differences do not exist in consumers' opinion seeking behavior in social networking sites with respect to their occupation.	**Not Supported**
H_0O-OP	Significant differences do not exist in consumers' opinion passing behavior in social networking sites with respect to their occupation.	**Supported**

Based on the above results, two sub hypotheses are supported. This result implies that, the main hypothesis *"**H_0O-EWOM:** Significant differences do not exist in consumers' electronic word of mouth behavior in social networking sites with respect to their occupation"*, is supported.

Electronic word of mouth behavior does not get influenced by occupation, as social network users who pass or seek opinion can be from any occupation. This word of mouth, is free of cost, and can be easily conveyed through social platforms.

Table 4.80: Summary of Mean Values of Electronic Word of Mouth Behavior w.r.t Occupation

Highest Education/SR	Opinion Leading	Opinion Seeking	Opinion Passing
Student	2.65	2.96	3.21
Service	2.54	2.82	3.06
Self Employed	2.72	2.76	3.11
Home Maker	2.00	2.00	2.50
Retired/Not Working/Others	2.05	1.95	2.40

As per table 4.80, the mean values amongst opinion leading and opinion seeking are less than 3 in all age groups. The respondents in in all the age groups show somewhat favorable attitude and behavior towards opinion passing behavior in social networking sites. The highest mean value (3.21) is acquired by respondents in the group, "Student", for opinion passing behavior.

The mean values of opinion passing behavior show highest value amongst all electronic word of mouth behavior behaviors.

4.5 SEM Results: Social Relationships and Electronic Word of Mouth Behavior of Consumers in Social Networking Sites

The structural equation modeling (SEM) approach was used to validate the research model. This approach was chosen because of its ability to test casual relationships between constructs with multiple measurement items.

Table 4.81: SEM Results

Electronic Word of Mouth Behavior		**Social Relationship Variable**	**Estimate**	**S.E.**	**C.R.**	**P**
Opinion Leading	<---	Normative Influence	.404	.053	7.635	***
Opinion Seeking	<---	Normative Influence	.370	.053	6.931	***
Opinion Passing	<---	Normative Influence	.233	.051	4.548	***
Opinion Leading	<---	Trust	.163	.052	3.143	.002
Opinion Seeking	<---	Trust	.149	.053	2.788	.005
Opinion Leading	<---	Social Capital	.186	.080	2.320	.020
Opinion Seeking	<---	Social Capital	.248	.083	2.981	.003
Opinion Passing	<---	Social Capital	.338	.083	4.049	***
Opinion Leading	<---	Informational Influence	.214	.045	4.806	***
Opinion Seeking	<---	Informational Influence	.377	.047	8.013	***
Opinion Passing	<---	Informational Influence	.265	.046	5.794	***
Opinion Passing	<---	Attitude Homophily	-.138	.054	-2.574	.010
Opinion Leading	<---	Background Homophily	.181	.060	3.030	.002
Opinion Seeking	<---	Background Homophily	.147	.061	2.388	.017
Opinion Passing	<---	Background Homophily	.179	.061	2.950	.003
Opinion Passing	<---	Tie Strength	.056	.057	.972	.331
Opinion Seeking	<---	Attitude Homophily	-.109	.054	-2.013	.044
Opinion Leading	<---	Attitude Homophily	-.053	.053	-1.018	.309
Opinion Passing	<---	Trust	.040	.052	.757	.449
Opinion Seeking	<---	Tie Strength	.042	.058	.717	.473
Opinion Leading	<---	Tie Strength	-.005	.056	-.081	.935

*****= significance smaller than .001**

Critical ratio (CR) is >1.96, then the path is significant at .05

A total of 16 paths have significant parameter estimates, from the above table.

1. Social Capital to Opinion Leading
2. Social Capital to Opinion Seeking
3. Social Capital to Opinion Passing
4. Trust to Opinion Leading
5. Trust to Opinion Seeking
6. Attitude Homophily to Opinion Seeking
7. Attitude Homophily to Opinion Passing
8. Background Homophily to Opinion Leading
9. Background Homophily to Opinion Seeking
10. Background Homophily to Opinion Passing
11. Normative Influence to Opinion Leading
12. Normative Influence to Opinion Seeking
13. Normative Influence to Opinion Passing
14. Informational Influence to Opinion Leading
15. Informational Influence to Opinion Seeking
16. Informational Influence to Opinion Passing

Table 4.82: Summary of Hypothesis Results

	Hypotheses	Critical Ratio	Probability Level	Results
H_0SC-OL	There is no significant impact of social capital on opinion leading behavior on social networking sites.	2.320	**.020**	**Not Supported**
H_0SC-OS	There is no significant impact of social capital on opinion seeking behavior on social networking sites.	2.981	**.003**	**Not Supported**
H_0SC-OP	There is no significant impact of social capital on opinion passing behavior on social networking sites.	4.049	***	**Not Supported**
H_0TS-OL	There is no significant impact of tie strength on opinion leading behavior on social networking sites.	-.081	.935	**Supported**
H_0TS-OS	There is no significant impact of tie strength on opinion seeking behavior on social networking sites.	.717	.473	**Supported**

H_0TS-OP	There is no significant impact of tie strength on opinion passing behavior on social networking sites.	.972	.331	**Supported**
H_0AH-OL	There is no significant impact of attitude homophily on opinion leading behavior on social networking sites.	-1.018	.309	**Supported**
H_0AH-OS	There is no significant impact of attitude homophily on opinion seeking behavior on social networking sites.	-2.013	**.044**	**Not Supported**
H_0AH-OP	There is no significant impact of attitude homophily on opinion passing behavior on social networking sites.	-2.574	**.010**	**Not Supported**
H_0BH-OL	There is no significant impact of background homophily on opinion leading behavior on social networking sites.	3.030	**.002**	**Not Supported**
H_0BH-OS	There is no significant impact of background homophily on opinion seeking behavior on social networking sites.	2.388	**.017**	**Not Supported**
H_0BH-OP	There is no significant impact of background homophily on opinion passing behavior on social networking sites.	2.950	**.003**	**Not Supported**
H_0TR-OL	There is no significant impact of trust on opinion leading behavior on social networking sites.	3.143	**.002**	**Not Supported**
H_0TR-OS	There is no significant impact of trust on opinion seeking behavior on social networking sites.	2.788	**.005**	**Not Supported**
H_0TR-OP	There is no significant impact of trust on opinion passing behavior on social networking sites.	.757	.449	**Supported**
H_0NI-OL	There is no significant impact of normative influence on opinion leading behavior on social networking sites.	7.635	***	**Not Supported**
H_0NI-OS	There is no significant impact of normative influence on opinion seeking behavior on social networking sites.	6.931	***	**Not Supported**
H_0NI-OP	There is no significant impact of normative influence on opinion passing behavior on social networking sites.	4.548	***	**Not Supported**

H_0II-OL	There is no significant impact of informational influence on opinion leading behavior on social networking sites.	4.806	***	**Not Supported**
H_0II-OS	There is no significant impact of informational influence on opinion seeking behavior on social networking sites.	8.013	***	**Not Supported**
H_0II-OP	There is no significant impact of informational influence on opinion passing behavior on social networking sites.	5.794	***	**Not Supported**

It was concluded that Social Capital, Background Homophily, Normative Influence, Informational Influence emerged to be strong significant predictors of electronic word of mouth, as all the three respective sub hypotheses were not supported in these four variables.

Null hypotheses related to Attitude Homophily and Trust were partially not supported, as two of the three respective sub hypotheses were not supported.

Only Tie Strength was not found to be a significant predictor, as all the respective null hypotheses were supported.

Criteria used to find significance:

Critical ratio (CR) is >1.96, then the path is significant at .05

*Probability values showing *** means that the significance is smaller than .001*

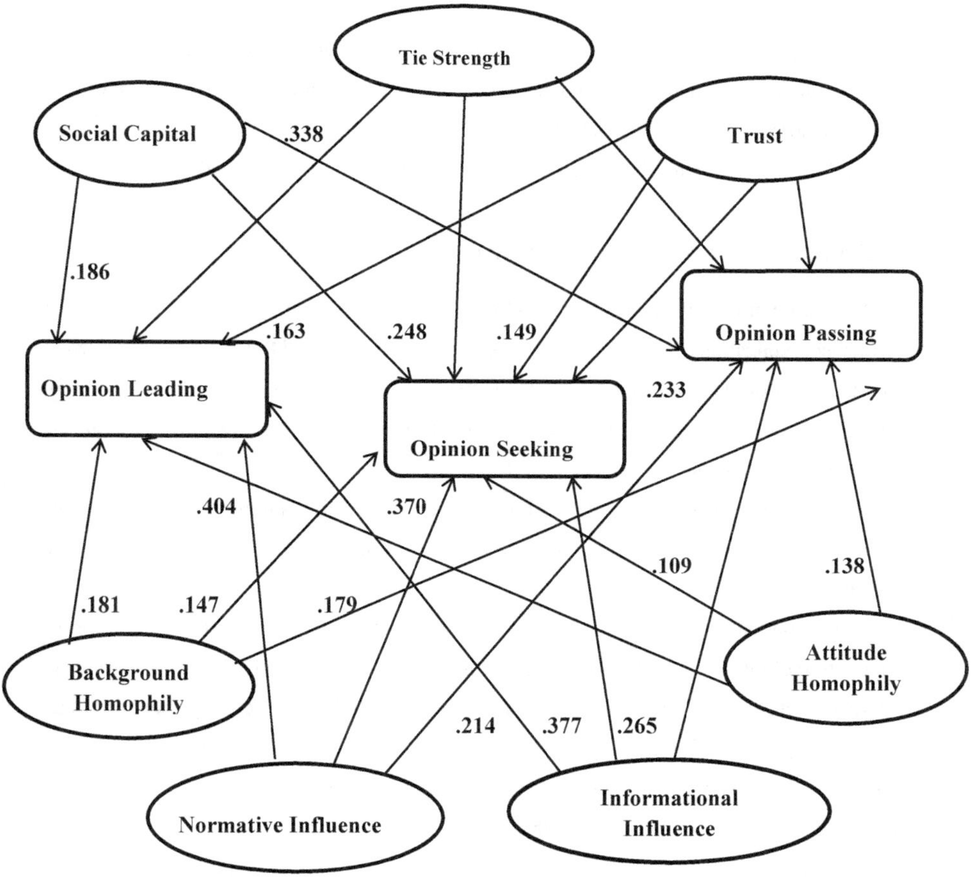

Fig. 4.1 Results from Testing Proposed SEM Model

The above figure indicates that sixteen hypothesized relationships are significant. These are the arrows with numbers on them. The numbers are like regression coefficients and are called path coefficients. Arrows with no numbers indicate that the path specified by that arrow is not significant.

4.6 Use of Social Networks within Organizations

To study the organizational differences in all the variables, analysis of variance (ANOVA) was applied to examine the difference in means. LSD Post-Hoc comparisons were carried out to confirm where the differences occurred between groups.

Descriptives have been calculated separately for each sector, as mentioned below.

4.6.1 Descriptive Analysis Sector wise

4.6.1.1 Descriptive Analysis - FMCG (Fast Moving Consumer Goods)

Brands/organizations in FMCG sector use television (M=4.82) for marketing communication, to a very large extent, followed by digital (M=4.26) and print (M=4.06). However, radio seems not to be favoured much by brands in FMCG sector, though the trend is picking up now.

Most of the brands in FMCG have started the use of social media within two years. The brands were very prominent on Facebook (M=4.42) followed by YouTube (M=3.72), and Twitter (M=3.36).

It was observed that companies have started allocating budget for new media forms, though traditional forms of communication are still highly budgeted. Most of the brands in FMCG sector had an approximate budget between 6 to 9% to be presently spent on social networking sites and other social media platforms. More than 80% of the brands manage and monitor social networking sites pages very frequently (M=4.68).

Sales promotion (M=4.40), providing product information (M=4.24) and integrating current ad campaign in the social media (M=4.20), are the most important purposes for which brands have considered using social networking sites. Ecommerce (M=2.62), recruitment (M=1.24), information about channel/dealerships (M=1.14) are not very popular purposes for which social media is used in organizations.

The important metrics deployed to evaluate success of social networking sites in FMCG brands were: Brand awareness (M=4.48), growth in number of participants (M=4.00), impact on sentiments and opinion (M=3.94), mention and prominence in relevant conversations (M=3.90) and increased engagement scores (M= 3.90).

E commerce revenues (M= 2.88) and cocreation of products and services are (M=3.02) are not widely used, when it comes to finalize metrics to evaluate success rates of social networking sites.

4.6.1.2 Descriptive Analysis -Automobiles

Brands in automotive sector use a combination of various media forms as print (M=4.77), digital (M=4.23), outdoors (M=4.19) and television (M=4.10).

Most of the brands in this sector have started the use of social media within 2-3 years.

The brands were very prominent on Facebook (M=4.39), followed by YouTube (M=3.81), and Twitter (M=3.61). Blogs (M=3.45) are used by brands, as word of mouth forms an integral part in purchase decisions, and consumers like to read product reviews. Most of the brands in this sector had an approximate budget between 9 to 12 per cent to be presently spent on social networking sites and other social media platforms.

Frequent tracking of social networking sites pages is very crucial, if brands want to enhance the effectiveness of new media. Around 80% of the brands manage and monitor social networking sites pages very frequently (M=4.35).

The survey revealed that sales promotion (M=4.00), providing product information (M= 4.42) and launching new products (M=3.90) were the main purposes for which social networking sites are used. The less popular purposes for which social media is used within organizations, are recruitment (M=1.13), information about channel/dealerships (M=2.52) and ecommerce (M=2.77). Automotive sector considers most of the metrics to evaluate effectiveness of social networking sites, major ones include: brand awareness (M=4.71), impact on sales (M=4.03), growth in participants (M=4.00) and competitors' insight (M=4.00).

4.6.1.3 Descriptive Analysis -Consumer Electronics/Home Appliances

There is a great use of print (M=4.50) and television (4.20) for promoting the brands, followed by digital medium (M=4.07). Around fifty per cent of the brands surveyed, have been engaged in social media initiatives for last three years.

The brands were very prominent on Facebook (M=4.10) followed by Twitter (3.20) and YouTube (M=3.10). Most of the brands in this sector had an approximate budget between 6 to 9% to be presently spent on social networking sites and other social media platforms.

Around 65% of the brands manage and monitor social networking sites pages very frequently (M=4.00).

The most important reasons of using social networks in marketing communication are: providing product information (M=4.10), sales promotion (M=3.97), speedy redressal of grievances (M=3.77) and faster replies to feedback (M=3.77).

Recruitment (M=1.10) and dealer information (M=2.40) are not considered to be very important, as of now.

The metrics which hold more value to track effectiveness are brand awareness (M=4.17), growth in participants (M=3.80), customer satisfaction score (M=3.80), impact on sentiment and opinion (M= 3.77) and insights of customers and competitors (M=3.77).

E- commerce revenues (M=2.73) was not considered important for evaluating success rates of social networking sites.

4.6.1.4 Descriptive Analysis –Banks, Financial Services and Insurance

Print (M=4.23) is the most preferred marketing channel along with digital (M=4.00) and television (M=3.96). Companies have been implementing social media for last two-three years.

Amongst social media channels, Facebook (M=4.00) emerged to be the most favourite, where brands want their presence to be felt.

Communication budget includes funds for social networks for reaching out customers. The brands track their social network pages frequently (M= 4.08) to have a better control over social media usage.

Providing product information (M=4.19), speedy redressal of grievances (M= 3.92), two way communication (M= 3.88) and faster replies to feedback (M=3.88) appeared to be the important purposes of using social networks. Recruitment (M=1.77), information about dealers (M= 2.23), ecommerce (2.77) don't seem to be lucrative purposes.

Metrics that are mostly used to evaluate success of social networks are brand awareness (M=4.12), customer satisfaction score (M=3.81) and impact on sentiment and opinion (M=3.73).

Ecommerce revenues (M=2.92) and cocreation of products and services (M=2.92) are the least preferred metrics.

4.6.2 Variations in Use of Various Forms of Marketing Communication Channels across Different Sectors

The table 4.83 shows the descriptives and ANOVA results for various forms of marketing communication channels across different sectors. The various forms include traditional media like print, TV, radio, outdoors as well as new media platforms. The mean values of various forms of marketing communication channels used in FMCG, AUTO, CE/HA and BFSI are 3.91, 4.09, 3.70 and 3.91 respectively. This shows that all the four sectors use various marketing communication tools to a good extent.

Table 4.83: Variations in Use of Various Forms of Marketing Communication Channels across Different Sectors

Sector	N	Mean	Std. Deviation	F	Significance	Remark
FMCG	50	3.91	.385	**1.838**	**.143**	**Not Significant**
AUTO	31	4.09	.449			
CE/HA	30	3.70	.669			
BFSI	26	3.91	.577			
Total	137	3.93	.515			

The results of ANOVA, as shown above shows that significant difference do not exist for use of various forms of marketing communication channels across different sectors (F=1.838, sig. = .143). Since the associated probability is more than the significance level of 0.05, the null hypothesis *"$H_0 1$: There is no significant difference in use of various forms of marketing communication channels across different sectors"* is supported.

Overall, the mean of total responses came out to be 3.93, which exhibits a strong positive use of marketing communication tools by brands.

Across four sectors, various tools of marketing communication do not show significant differences, so it can be concluded that the importance of various form is imminent in all sectors. There is an integration of new media into traditional media, so marketers need to implement their MARCOM programme efficiently.

Table 4.84: Multiple Comparisons of Use of Various Forms of Marketing Communication Channels across Different Sectors

(I) Industry	(J) Industry	Mean Difference (I-J)	Sig.	Remark
FMCG	**AUTO**	-.1808	.124	**Not Significant**
	CE/HA	.1227	.300	**Not Significant**
	BFSI	.0006	.996	**Not Significant**
AUTO	**FMCG**	.1808	.124	**Not Significant**
	CE/HA	.3034*	.022	**Significant**
	BFSI	.1814	.184	**Not Significant**
CE/HA	**FMCG**	-.1227	.300	**Not Significant**
	AUTO	-.3034*	.022	**Significant**
	BFSI	-.1221	.374	**Not Significant**
BFSI	**FMCG**	-.0006	.996	**Not Significant**
	AUTO	-.1814	.184	**Not Significant**
	CE/HA	.1221	.374	**Not Significant**

*. The mean difference is significant at the 0.05 level.

The above comparison shows that only one paired groups show significant relationships. Significant differences were observed between Auto and Consumer Electronics/Home Appliances (p= .022).

It has been observed that marketing and advertising expenses have increased in automotive sector, due to launch of new brands on a frequent basis. So, we see that all forms of marketing communication have been efficiently utilized by auto industries. Last year we saw the aggressive social media advertising of Ford Eco sport, a new SUV which was launched around mid-2013. Brands are integrating new media into the traditional forms for reaching right target audience at a lesser cost.

Moreover, the number of brands launched under automotive sector is less in number as compared to those launched under consumer durables category.

4.6.3 Variations in Years of Engagement through Social Media Channels Across Different Sectors

The table 4.85 shows the descriptives and ANOVA results for various forms of marketing communication channels across different sectors. The mean values of years of engagement through social media channels in FMCG, AUTO, CE/HA and BFSI are 2.68, 2.68, 2.70 and 2.65 respectively. This shows that all the four sectors have been engaged in various marketing communication tools for not very long.

Table 4.85: Variations in Years of Engagement through Social Media Channels across Different Sectors

Sector	N	Mean	Std. Deviation	F	Significance	Remark
FMCG	50	2.68	1.096	.009	.999	**Not Significant**
AUTO	31	2.68	.979			
CE/HA	30	2.70	.877			
BFSI	26	2.65	1.129			
Total	137	2.68	1.021			

The results of ANOVA, as shown above shows that significant difference does not exist in years of engagement through social media channels across different sectors (F=.009, sig. = .999). Since the associated probability is more than the significance level of 0.05, the null hypothesis *"$H_0$2: There is no significant difference in years of engagement through social media channels across different sectors"* is supported.

The use of social networks in marketing communication is not a very old phenomenon, though many social networking sites already exist since a decade.

Most of the social media savvy organizations have implemented social networks within last 2-3 years. The result as above indicates that, still there are opportunities for brands to give more importance to new media.

Many public sector and government organizations are still reluctant to use social networks for marketing and advertising, as they have not realized its importance.

Across four sectors, no significant differences were found in the years of engagement through social media channels. Many brands initially used blogs to start interacting with customers, but emerging forms of social networks i.e. Facebook, LinkedIn can provide more user friendly and better interactive platform.

Table 4.86: Multiple Comparisons of Years of Engagement through Social Media Channels across Different Sectors

(I) Industry	(J) Industry	Mean Difference (I-J)	Sig.	Remark
FMCG	AUTO	.003	.991	Not Significant
	CE/HA	-.020	.933	Not Significant
	BFSI	.026	.917	Not Significant
AUTO	FMCG	-.003	.991	Not Significant
	CE/HA	-.023	.932	Not Significant
	BFSI	.024	.932	Not Significant
CE/HA	FMCG	.020	.933	Not Significant
	AUTO	.023	.932	Not Significant
	BFSI	.046	.868	Not Significant
BFSI	FMCG	-.026	.917	Not Significant
	AUTO	-.024	.932	Not Significant
	CE/HA	-.046	.868	Not Significant

No significant differences were observed between any paired groups. The results showed no variations in years of engagement through social media channels across different sectors.

The results as shown in Table 4.86 strongly support the hypothesis that there is no difference in years of engagement.

4.6.4 Variations in Use of Various Forms of Social Media Channels across Different Sectors

The table 4.87 shows the descriptives and ANOVA results for various forms of marketing communication channels across different sectors. The mean values of use of various forms of social media channels in FMCG, AUTO, CE/HA and BFSI are 2.86, 3.17, 2.83 and 2.79 respectively. This shows that all the four sectors have been somewhat engaged in various forms of social media channels.

Table 4.87: Variations in Use of Various Forms of Social Media Channels across Different Sectors

Sector	N	Mean	Std. Deviation	F	Significance	Remark
FMCG	50	2.86	.334	**4.015**	**.009**	**Significant**
AUTO	31	3.17	.460			
CE/HA	30	2.83	.612			
BFSI	26	2.79	.611			
Total	137	2.91	.507			

The results of ANOVA, as shown above shows that significant difference exists in use of various forms of social media channels across different sectors (F=4.015, sig. = .009). Since the associated probability is less than the significance level of 0.05, the null hypothesis *"$H_0$3: There is no significant difference in use of various forms of social media channels across different sectors"* is not supported.

The various forms of social media channels used are Company blog, Facebook, Twitter, Linked In, You Tube, Pinterest, Yahoo, Wikipedia, Google+, etc.

Table 4.88: Multiple Comparisons of Use of Various Forms of Social Media Channels across Different Sectors

(I) Industry	(J) Industry	Mean Difference (I-J)	Sig.	Remark
FMCG	AUTO	-.316*	.005	**Significant**
	CE/HA	.028	.799	**Not Significant**
	BFSI	.071	.547	**Not Significant**
AUTO	FMCG	.316*	.005	**Significant**
	CE/HA	.345*	.007	**Significant**
	BFSI	.388*	.003	**Significant**
CE/HA	FMCG	-.028	.799	**Not Significant**
	AUTO	-.345*	.007	**Significant**
	BFSI	.042	.746	**Not Significant**
BFSI	FMCG	-.071	.547	**Not Significant**
	AUTO	-.388*	.003	**Significant**
	CE/HA	-.042	.746	**Not Significant**
*.The mean difference is significant at the 0.05 level.				

Three of the paired groups showed significant differences.

AUTO showed significant differences with all other three sectors-Fast Moving Consumer Goods, Consumer Electronics/Home Appliances, Banking, Financial Services and Insurance. It has been seen in recent years that automotive sector has become very competitive, and there are number of international brands, present in the Indian market. So, there is a need for the brands to devise innovative marketing communication programs.

4.6.5 Variations in Budget Allotted to Social Networking Sites across Different Sectors

The table 4.89 shows the descriptives and ANOVA results for budget allotted to social networking sites across different sectors. The mean values of budget allotted to social networking sites in FMCG, AUTO, CE/HA and BFSI are 3.14, 3.29, 2.90 and 3.08 respectively. This shows that all the four sectors have somewhat allocated moderate budget on social media.

Table 4.89: Variations in Budget Allotted to Social Networking Sites across Different Sectors

Sector	N	Mean	Std. Deviation	F	Significance	Remark
FMCG	50	3.14	.670	**.867**	**.460**	**Not Significant**
AUTO	31	3.29	.783			
CE/HA	30	2.90	1.348			
BFSI	26	3.08	1.093			
Total	137	3.11	.960			

The results of ANOVA, as shown above shows that significant difference does not exist in use of various forms of social media channels across different sectors (F=.867, sig. = .460). Since the associated probability is more than the significance level of 0.05, the null hypothesis *"$H_0$4: There is no significant difference in budget allotted to social networking sites across different sector"* is supported.

Table 4.90: Multiple Comparisons of Budget allotted to Social Networking Sites across Different Sectors

(I) Industry	(J) Industry	Mean Difference (I-J)	Sig.	Remark
FMCG	AUTO	-.150	.495	Not Significant
	CE/HA	.240	.282	Not Significant
	BFSI	.063	.787	Not Significant
AUTO	FMCG	.150	.495	Not Significant
	CE/HA	.390	.115	Not Significant
	BFSI	.213	.405	Not Significant
CE/HA	FMCG	-.240	.282	Not Significant
	AUTO	-.390	.115	Not Significant
	BFSI	-.177	.493	Not Significant
BFSI	FMCG	-.063	.787	Not Significant
	AUTO	-.213	.405	Not Significant
	CE/HA	.177	.493	Not Significant

All the paired groups are not significant as concluded from LSD Post Hoc test. The mean differences were found to be highly insignificant.

It can be inferred that the integration of social networks in marketing communication is not an old phenomenon, so the budget allocation towards this part is still not very high, as compared to traditional forms of advertising.

4.6.5 Variations in Frequency of Managing Social Networking Sites across Different Sectors

The table 4.91 shows the descriptives and ANOVA results for frequency of managing social networking sites across different sectors. The mean values of budget allotted to social networking sites in FMCG, AUTO, CE/HA and BFSI are 4.68, 4.35, 4.00 and 4.08 respectively. This shows that all the four sectors have started integrating social media channels and at the same time, they are taking this seriously, through proper execution and monitoring.

Table 4.91: Variations in Frequency of Managing Social Networking Sites across Different Sectors

Sector	N	Mean	Std. Deviation	F	Significance	Remark
FMCG	50	4.68	.844			
AUTO	31	4.35	1.279			
CE/HA	30	4.00	1.365	**2.787**	**.043**	**Significant**
BFSI	26	4.08	1.230			
Total	137	4.34	1.172			

The results of ANOVA, as shown above shows that a significant difference exists in frequency of managing social networking sites across different sectors (F=2.787, sig. = .043). Since the associated probability is less than the significance level of 0.05, the null hypothesis *"**$H_0$5**: There is no significant difference in frequency of managing social networking sites across different sectors"* is not supported.

Many of the global brands actively monitor their brand pages and maintain a proper online reputation management. Significant differences can be seen in the frequency of managing brand pages, as it was observed that public companies are less active on social networks as compared to private companies. Banks and Financial services were less active in comparison to other sectors.

Table 4.92: Multiple Comparisons of Frequency of Managing Social Networking Sites across Different Sectors

(I) Industry	(J) Industry	Mean Difference (I-J)	Sig.	Remark
FMCG	AUTO	.325	.218	**Not Significant**
	CE/HA	.680*	.012	**Significant**
	BFSI	.603*	.032	**Significant**
AUTO	FMCG	-.325	.218	**Not Significant**
	CE/HA	.355	.230	**Not Significant**
	BFSI	.278	.365	**Not Significant**
CE/HA	FMCG	-.680*	.012	**Significant**
	AUTO	-.355	.230	**Not Significant**
	BFSI	-.077	.803	**Not Significant**
BFSI	FMCG	-.603*	.032	**Significant**
	AUTO	-.278	.365	**Not Significant**
	CE/HA	.077	.803	**Not Significant**
*. The mean difference is significant at the 0.05 level.				

Two of the paired groups show significance as concluded from LSD Post Hoc test. FMCG showed significant differences with CE/HA and BFSI.

4.6.6 Variations in the Purposes for which Social Networking Sites are used across Different Sectors

The table 4.93 shows the descriptives and ANOVA results for frequency of managing social networking sites across different sectors. The mean values purposes for which social networking sites are used across different sectors in FMCG, AUTO, CE/HA AND BFSI are 3.42, 3.44, 3.35 and 3.32 respectively.

Table 4.93: Variations in Purposes for which Social Networking Sites are used across Different Sectors

Sector	N	Mean	Std. Deviation	F	Significance	Remark
FMCG	50	3.42	.844	**.529**	**.663**	**Not Significant**
AUTO	31	3.44	1.279			
CE/HA	30	3.35	1.365			
BFSI	26	3.32	1.230			
Total	137	3.39	1.172			

The results of ANOVA, as shown above shows that a significant difference exists in purposes for which social networking sites are used across different sectors (F=.529, sig. = .663). Since the associated probability is more than the significance level of 0.05, the null hypothesis *"$H_0$6: There is no significant difference in the purposes for which social networking sites are used across different sectors"* is supported.

All four sectors have mean values greater than 3, which imply that brands have fixed purposes in their social media strategies.

Table 4.94: Multiple Comparisons of Purposes for which Social Networking Sites are used across Different Sectors

(I) Industry	(J) Industry	Mean Difference (I-J)	Sig.	Remark
FMCG	**AUTO**	-.020	.842	**Not Significant**
	CE/HA	.075	.473	**Not Significant**
	BFSI	.102	.347	**Not Significant**
AUTO	**FMCG**	.020	.842	**Not Significant**
	CE/HA	.095	.410	**Not Significant**
	BFSI	.123	.305	**Not Significant**
CE/HA	**FMCG**	-.075	.473	**Not Significant**
	AUTO	-.095	.410	**Not Significant**
	BFSI	.027	.818	**Not Significant**
BFSI	**FMCG**	-.102	.347	**Not Significant**
	AUTO	-.123	.305	**Not Significant**
	CE/HA	-.027	.818	**Not Significant**

The means of all the paired groups show non-significant differences. This means that all sectors are taking into consideration, the various purposes for which social networking sites are used within marketing communication program.

4.6.7 Variations in Metrics Deployed to Evaluate Effectiveness of Social Networking Sites, across Different Sectors

The table 4.95 shows the descriptives and ANOVA results for frequency of managing social networking sites across different sectors. The mean values purposes for which social networking sites are used across different sectors in FMCG, AUTO, CE/HA AND BFSI are 3.42, 3.44, 3.35 and 3.32 respectively.

Table 4.95: Variations in Metrics Deployed to Evaluate Effectiveness of Social Networking Sites across Different Sectors

Sector	N	Mean	Std. Deviation	F	Significance	Remark
FMCG	50	3.56	.373	.642	.590	Not Significant
AUTO	31	3.72	.356			
CE/HA	30	3.59	.615			
BFSI	26	3.62	.712			
Total	137	3.61	.505			

The results of ANOVA, as shown above shows that a significant difference does not exist in metrics deployed to evaluate effectiveness of social networking sites, across different sectors (F=.642, sig. = .590). Since the associated probability is more than the significance level of 0.05, the null hypothesis *"**$H_0$7**: There is no significant difference in metrics deployed to evaluate effectiveness of social networking sites, across different sectors"* is supported.

The mean values across all four sectors are greater than 3, so it can be inferred that brands across various sectors have implemented metrics for evaluating the effectiveness of social networks.

Table 4.96: Multiple Comparisons of Metrics Deployed to Evaluate Effectiveness of Social Networking Sites across Different Sectors

(I) Industry	(J) Industry	Mean Difference (I-J)	Sig.	Remark
FMCG	AUTO	-.156	.179	Not Significant
	CE/HA	-.025	.829	Not Significant
	BFSI	-.052	.670	Not Significant
AUTO	FMCG	.156	.179	Not Significant
	CE/HA	.131	.314	Not Significant
	BFSI	.104	.442	Not Significant
CE/HA	FMCG	.025	.829	Not Significant
	AUTO	-.131	.314	Not Significant
	BFSI	-.027	.842	Not Significant
BFSI	FMCG	.052	.670	Not Significant
	AUTO	-.104	.442	Not Significant
	CE/HA	.027	.842	Not Significant

The means of all the paired groups show non-significant differences. This means that all sectors have started using a combination of metrics to calculate the return on investment.

Table 4.97: Summary of Hypotheses Testing Results based on Use of Social Networks within Organizations

	Hypothesis	Result
$H_0 1$	There is no significant difference in use of various forms of marketing communication channels across different sectors.	**Supported**
$H_0 2$	There is no significant difference in years of engagement through social media channels across different sectors.	**Supported**
$H_0 3$	There is no significant difference in use of various forms of social media channels across different sectors.	**Not Supported**
$H_0 4$	There is no significant difference in budget allotted to social networking sites across different sectors.	**Supported**
$H_0 5$	There is no significant difference in frequency of managing social networking sites across different sectors.	**Not Supported**
$H_0 6$	There is no significant difference in the purposes for which social networking sites are used across different sectors.	**Supported**
$H_0 7$	There is no significant difference in metrics deployed to evaluate effectiveness of social networking sites across different sectors	**Supported**

All the select sectors have been using a combination of traditional media and new media. The marketers need to address the issue of integration of various media forms. Significant differences were observed in use of various social media platforms like social networks (Facebook, Linked In), You Tube, Blogs, etc.

The results showed a significant difference in frequency of managing social networking sites by sectors covered in the study.

Printed by BoD™in Norderstedt, Germany

9 781836 561606